Teaching Students to Use AI Ethically & Responsibly

Teaching Students to Use AI Ethically & Responsibly

Exploring AI With Intentionality, Curiosity, and Care

Salman Khan

Douglas Fisher

Nancy Frey

James Marshall

Meghan Hargrave

CORWIN

FOR INFORMATION:

Corwin

A SAGE Company

2455 Teller Road

Thousand Oaks, California 91320

(800) 233-9936

www.corwin.com

SAGE Publications Ltd.

1 Oliver's Yard

55 City Road

London EC1Y 1SP

United Kingdom

SAGE Publications India Pvt. Ltd.

Unit No 323-333, Third Floor, F-Block

International Trade Tower Nehru Place

New Delhi 110 019

India

SAGE Publications Asia-Pacific Pte. Ltd.

18 Cross Street #10–10/11/12

China Square Central

Singapore 048423

Vice President and Editorial Director: Monica Eckman

Senior Director and Publisher, Content and Product: Lisa Luedeke

Content Development Editor: Sarah Ross

Product Associate: Zachary Vann

Production Editor: Tracy Buyan

Typesetter: C&M Digitals (P) Ltd.

Proofreader: Heather Kerrigan

Indexer: Integra

Graphic Designer: Rose Storey

Marketing Manager: Megan Naidl

Copyright © 2026 by Corwin Press, Inc.

All rights reserved. Except as permitted by U.S. copyright law, no part of this work may be reproduced or distributed in any form or by any means, or stored in a database or retrieval system, without permission in writing from the publisher.

When forms and sample documents appearing in this work are intended for reproduction, they will be marked as such. Reproduction of their use is authorized for educational use by educators, local school sites, and/or noncommercial or nonprofit entities that have purchased the book.

All third-party trademarks referenced or depicted herein are included solely for the purpose of illustration and are the property of their respective owners. Reference to these trademarks in no way indicates any relationship with, or endorsement by, the trademark owner.

No AI training. Without in any way limiting the author's and publisher's exclusive rights under copyright, any use of this publication to "train" generative artificial intelligence (AI) or for other AI uses is expressly prohibited. The publisher reserves all rights to license uses of this publication for generative AI training or other AI uses.

ISBN 9798348832223 (spiral)

Library of Congress Control Number: 2025941928

DISCLAIMER: This book may direct you to access third-party content via web links, QR codes, or other scannable technologies, which are provided for your reference by the author(s). Corwin makes no guarantee that such third-party content will be available for your use and encourages you to review the terms and conditions of such third-party content. Corwin takes no responsibility and assumes no liability for your use of any third-party content, nor does Corwin approve, sponsor, endorse, verify, or certify such third-party content.

CONTENTS

About the Authors ix

INTRODUCTION 1

SECTION 1. TEACHING *ABOUT* AI: "UNDER THE HOOD" CONCEPTS TO SUPPORT GOOD, ETHICAL, EFFECTIVE USE OF AI FOR LEARNING 5

    Overview 5

GENERATIVE MODELS 7

PERSONALIZED MASTERY-BASED LEARNING 12

HUMAN-IN-THE-LOOP EXPERIENCES 17

COLLECTIVE INTELLIGENCE 22

ADAPTIVE PLATFORMS 27

AI, DATA, AND YOU 32

AI LIMITATIONS 36

AI AND SOCIETY 41

SECTION 2. TEACHING *FOR* AI: DEVELOPING HUMAN INTELLIGENCE SKILLS IN STUDENTS 45

    Overview 45

INFORMATION LITERACY 48

DATA LITERACY 52

QUESTIONING 56

PROMPT ENGINEERING 61

DIALOGUE 65

VERIFICATION 71

CRITICAL INTERPRETATION 76

CURIOSITY 80

METACOGNITION 84

COGNITIVE FLEXIBILITY 90

ETHICAL REASONING 95

SELF-REGULATION 100

TEACHER DECISION-MAKING: WHEN STUDENTS CAN
USE AI (AND WHEN THEY CANNOT) 104

SECTION 3. TEACHING *WITH* AI: LEARNING QUESTS THAT IGNITE CURIOSITY AND DEEPEN UNDERSTANDING   109

    Overview   109

ANCHOR QUEST 111

CLARITY QUEST 115

COMPARE QUEST 119

CRITIQUE QUEST 123

GROWTH QUEST 127

LEVEL-UP QUEST 131

MISSION QUEST 135

PERSPECTIVE QUEST 139

REVERSE QUEST 143

RIGHT-SIZING QUEST 147

Conclusion	151
References	153
Index	159

Visit the companion website at
https://companion.corwin.com/courses/TeachingStudentsAI
for downloadable resources.

ABOUT THE AUTHORS

Salman Khan is the founder and CEO of the education nonprofit Khan Academy, which has the mission of "providing free, world-class education for anyone, anywhere." It has 180 million registered users in over 50 languages. Salman is also the author of *Brave New Words*, a book about the future of AI in education and *The One World Schoolhouse*.

Douglas Fisher is professor and chair of educational leadership at San Diego State University and a teacher leader at Health Sciences High and Middle College. Previously, Doug was an early intervention teacher and elementary school educator. He is a credentialed English teacher and administrator in California. In 2022, he was inducted into the Reading Hall of Fame by the Literacy Research Association. He has published numerous articles on reading and literacy, leadership, and curriculum design, as well as books such as *The Teacher Clarity Playbook* (2nd ed.), *Your Introduction to PLC+*, *The Illustrated Guide to Teacher Credibility*, *Instructional Strategies to Move Learning Forward: 50+ Tools That Support Gradual Release of Responsibility,* and *Welcome to Teaching!*

Nancy Frey is a professor in educational leadership at San Diego State University and a teacher leader at Health Sciences High and Middle College. She is a credentialed special educator, reading specialist, and administrator in California. She is a member of the International Literacy Association's Literacy Research Panel. Her published titles include *50 Strategies for Activating Your PLC+, The Illustrated Guide to Visible Learning, Welcome to Teaching Multilingual Learners, Teaching Foundational Skills to Adolescent Readers,* and *RIGOR Unveiled: A Video-Enhanced Flipbook to Promote Teacher Expertise in Relationship Building, Instruction, Goals, Organization, and Relevance.*

James Marshall is a professor of educational leadership at San Diego State University, where he also leads the Doctorate in Educational Leadership program. A credentialed teacher, he began his career as an informal science educator at the San Diego Zoo. Jim's passion centers on the design of learning programs that yield predictable results. He has written broadly on needs assessment, learning initiative design, implementation, and program evaluation. His published books include *Right From the Start: The Essential Guide to Implementing School Initiatives, Fixing Education Initiatives in Crisis: 24 Go-To Strategies,* and *RIGOR Unveiled: A Video-Enhanced Flipbook to Promote Teacher Expertise in Relationship Building, Instruction, Goals, Organization, and Relevance.*

ABOUT THE AUTHORS

Meghan Hargrave is an experienced educator, with over 15 years in the field. After being a teacher leader in the classroom, she moved into education coaching and consulting where she supports hundreds of K–12 schools and districts worldwide. Her work has always focused on important instructional shifts in education and practical ways the educators she supports can embrace these shifts effectively, which has included the integration of artificial intelligence tools in the classroom. She is ChatGPT, GoogleAI, and AI for Education certified in addition to working closely with thousands of educators on how to implement these tools in the classroom. She is author of *The Artificial Intelligence Playbook: Time-Saving Tools to Make Learning More Engaging* and is an international presenter, has taught preservice teachers at Columbia University's Teachers College, regularly contributes to popular educational publications, and is known for sharing innovative and effective classroom strategies via social media @letmeknowhowitgoes.

INTRODUCTION

Let's go whale-watching. Pack your sunscreen, snacks, and a pair of binoculars and let's set off on an adventure. We shove off early in the morning, a boat full of strangers, each of us hoping to spot something majestic breaching the ocean surface. An hour in, we're still watching and nothing. A low fog sits on the water. The guide cheerfully narrates each far-off sea lion as if it were a spectacle. A young person a few seats over keeps insisting that something is "just over there." Then suddenly, when we've all but given up, we see the tail. An unmistakable, gleaming arc that rises up, pauses, and vanishes again with impossible grace. It's enormous. Beautiful. And gone in seconds.

That's how teaching with artificial intelligence feels to many of us. Something massive is clearly surfacing in our work. It's powerful, sleek, and unpredictable. We see it in headlines and hear it in hallway conversations. Students ask about it. Our colleagues try it. Leaders reference it in ways that make you wonder if someone, somewhere, is expecting you to do something with it, and soon. Teaching for, with, and about AI to PK–12 students can be a little bit like the experience of trying to understand and engage with a whale, an awe-inspiring, complex, and deeply interconnected being. AI is not a living creature, but the parallels haven't escaped us:

1. **AI Is Massive but Mostly Hidden.** Like a whale, AI is huge, but most of its size is beneath the surface. Students need help understanding what's visible (like ChatGPT or image generators) and what's hidden (like algorithms, data collection, and infrastructure). You're not just seeing the tail splash. You're learning about the whole ecosystem below that.

2. **AI Is a Living System You Must Approach With Respect.** Whales are intelligent and powerful, but they require careful, ethical interaction. They can also tip your boat over! Similarly, AI must be approached responsibly. Students need to learn about bias, privacy, and the consequences of misuse. You don't tame a whale; you learn how to swim alongside it with humility while keeping safety in mind.

3. **You Can Learn From AI but Not Control It Fully.** Like studying whale behavior, students can explore and come to understand patterns in AI, but the outcomes are sometimes unpredictable or opaque. This requires that students learn to ask critical questions like, *Why did the AI do that? Can I trust it? How can I refine my interaction?*

4. **AI Requires Deep, Sustained Observation.** You don't understand a whale from witnessing one splash. You learn over time through patient observation, study, questioning, and reflection. Likewise, learning AI isn't about flashy tools. Instead, it's about developing a concept and understanding over time: data, modeling, ethics, application.

5. **AI Lives in an Interconnected Ecosystem.** Whales don't exist in isolation. They are part of a larger, interdependent ecosystem. AI is the same: It intersects with society, economy, equity, education, and environment. Teaching students about AI means showing its intersections and interdependence with the world around them.

6. **AI Can Inspire Awe and Wonder.** Encountering a whale often creates a sense of awe. AI, when taught well, can also ignite curiosity and creativity. Students can imagine new futures, solve real problems, and express themselves in new ways. Artificial intelligence will have an impact on human intelligence. Students need to know how to responsibly use AI while they develop their own thinking skills.

WHAT YOU'LL FIND IN THIS BOOK

We didn't write this book for AI evangelists. It also isn't written for skeptics waiting for AI to go away. It's written for educators standing on the deck, scanning the horizon, and wondering: *Is this for me? My students? How do we make sense of it? What happens if I do nothing? And what happens if I dive in but don't fully know what's beneath the surface?* This book serves as a guide to understanding, approaching, and using AI with all the intentionality, curiosity, and care we bring to everything else that matters in our classrooms. AI is enormous. But like any ecosystem, it can be explored. It can be mapped. It can be navigated. And eventually, it can be taught.

We've organized the contents into three major sections.

1. **Teaching *About* AI** explores the systems understanding, appropriate for various grade levels, about the AI systems themselves. This includes building foundational knowledge about what AI is, how it's created, how it makes decisions, and how it can be both useful and flawed. We're reminded of a friend who told us that it was not critical to understand how a fuel injection system works to drive a car. However, there are some aspects of how a vehicle works that are required to effectively drive and problem-solve as you drive, such as the turn signal versus the windshield wiper controls. Thus, this section includes topics such as generative models, personalized mastery-based learning, collective intelligence, and adaptive learning systems. These are all aspects of AI that students (and you) need to understand to use the information they gain. By equipping students with this foundational systems knowledge, we give them the tools to question, evaluate, and participate in the AI-driven world as informed, ethical, and empowered learners.

2. **Teaching *for* AI** focuses on the skills that students need to develop to successfully navigate an AI-influenced world. Many of these skills have been repurposed and updated, such as curiosity and questioning. Curiosity must now be directed not just at the natural world or texts, but also at how machines interpret information.

Questioning becomes more than a comprehension strategy as it's essential for interacting meaningfully with AI systems. Others are newer skills or skills that are specific to AI, such as prompt engineering and verification skills. Without these competencies, students risk becoming passive users of technology rather than critical thinkers and collaborators alongside it. This section focuses on the human intelligence that must continue to be developed for students to learn with and from AI in responsible and ethical ways. Teaching for AI is ultimately about preparing students not just to use AI tools, but to question, evaluate, and shape how those tools serve learning, decision-making, and society.

3. **Teaching *With* AI** turns our attention to the purposeful integration of AI in classroom instruction. When you understand the basics about how AI works and the skills we need to develop with students, you are ready to integrate AI into your teaching and students' learning. Of course, you still have other things to teach, concepts and skills that are represented in your grade-level standards. AI can help you with lesson planning, assessment design, and a variety of other teacher tasks, which we explored in the *Artificial Intelligence Playbook* (Hargrave et al., 2025). In this book, we focus on the use of AI in students' learning through a series of quests. When the internet in the classroom was new, an inquiry process called WebQuest was created to engage students in learning (Dodge, 1995). WebQuests were innovative for their time, guiding students through inquiry-based learning using internet resources. Now with AI and chatbots, there's an opportunity to design similarly structured experiences that leverage dialogue, personalization, and problem-solving through interaction. Thus, we have developed and tested 10 quests that invite students into learning with AI.

In these three sections, we explore 31 topics. These 31 topics will help you, the educator, support students as they learn and grow. *We think of this as using artificial intelligence to foster human intelligence.* Each of the topics includes a definition, an explanation about why it's important, classroom examples, and teacher and student practices. In addition, we see the topic in action in classrooms. And, taking our advice for using AI as a co-pilot and teacher assistant, we fed the content of each topic into our AI system (ChatGPT) and with several back-and-forth interactions on each topic, generated a skill progression across the grade bands with supports necessary for students to become successful. For each progression, we built out a handful of the supports, resulting in more than 120 online resources that can be used to support the teaching of each of these skills in PK–12 classrooms. These progressions, and the accompanying online supports, are a starting point for integrating AI into your classroom. Taken together, they represent a new form of literacy, AI Literacy. Here's a working definition:

> *AI literacy represents the technical knowledge, durable skills, and future-ready attitudes required to thrive in a world influenced by AI. It enables learners to engage, create with, manage, and design AI, while critically evaluating its benefits, risks, and ethical implications.*
> (OECD, 2025)

Teaching with AI and developing AI Literacy for your students isn't about chasing trends or fearing change. It's about learning to recognize something massive, powerful, and increasingly present in our classrooms. Like spotting a whale breaching the surface, AI can feel awe-inspiring and mysterious, sometimes overwhelming. But with patience, curiosity, and guidance, we can begin to understand what's beneath the surface and help our students do the same. Whether you're just getting your feet wet or already diving deep, we invite you to continue reading.

Let's navigate this together.

Section 1

Teaching *About* AI

"Under the Hood" Concepts to Support Good, Ethical, Effective Use of AI for Learning

OVERVIEW

The introduction suggested that teaching in the age of AI is like spotting a whale just beneath the surface. Its presence is unmistakable; massive, powerful, and at times unpredictable. This is the "about" section—the part that surfaces what AI is, how it works, and why it matters. This is not a technical manual but rather we provide information about the way that these systems work such that you can begin teaching students about AI.

Our students don't just use AI. They live in a world increasingly shaped by it. From autocorrect to adaptive learning platforms, from personalized playlists to AI-generated search results, the systems students interact with are constantly learning from them. Even still, students are rarely invited to understand how these systems operate, what they do with user data, or what values and assumptions they encode. Teaching about AI means giving students that knowledge and with it, the agency to ask better questions, make informed choices, and become responsible digital participants.

This section focuses on foundational concepts every learner should understand: how generative models make predictions, why adaptive platforms respond the way they do, what it means to be the "human in the loop," and how data fuels personalization and surveillance. It challenges students to think about where they encounter AI, what AI gets right, what it misses, and who decides how it's used. These are ethical, civic, and deeply human questions.

We want students to remain curious about AI. Just as we teach them to question texts, evaluate sources, and revise their own thinking, the same now applies to AI outputs. That means positioning AI as a tool that becomes more powerful when paired with thoughtful human use . . . rather than a "magic answer machine" or a "threat to learning."

In this section, you'll find ways to help students demystify AI, critique its limitations, reflect on how they learn, and engage in human–AI collaboration. Across the ideas presented, one thread is clear: Students should not be passive recipients of AI-generated content. They should be decision-makers, collaborators, and questioners—always keeping the human voice and human judgment at the center of their learning.

Like many complex systems of today's world, AI is mostly invisible. Its workings are hidden behind clean interfaces and seamless outputs. But when we take the time to look beneath the surface—and help students do the same—we make the invisible visible. And that's the heart of this section: to help students see what's really there, and to prepare them to think critically and use AI responsibly in a world where AI is part of the current, not just the splash.

Generative Models

WHAT IS IT?

Generative models are a type of AI designed to create unique responses to human input by using patterns and massive amounts of data it has been trained on. These models don't just respond, they generate. They can write, draw, solve problems, create videos, and even suggest personalized learning tasks.

WHY IT MATTERS

Generative models open up new possibilities for students as thinkers, creators, and problem-solvers. These tools can act like a thought partner to generate ideas, suggest wording, provide feedback, or even create visuals, images, videos, and podcasts. For students who feel stuck, generative AI can offer a jumpstart. For those who already have ideas, it can provide new ways to expand or refine them. By understanding what generative models are and what they can do, students can begin to approach assignments, projects, and creative tasks both in school and out with more flexibility and confidence. Additionally, this knowledge also helps students recognize when they're interacting with content created by AI, whether online, on social media, or even at school.

HOW IT WORKS

To help highlight how generative models work, it's useful to first understand how these tools differ from a basic search engine. Although generative models may seem similar to online platforms we've used for a long time, they operate in fundamentally different ways. A search engine returns links to existing web pages, relying heavily on keyword matching. This means users often have to phrase their query just right to get relevant results. Generative AI, on the other hand, produces new content based on patterns in its training data. It uses advanced natural language processing (NLP) to interpret meaning, nuance, and even conversational tone—making it more responsive to the user's intent rather than just the exact words used (Kimes, 2024). The result is a unique, user-guided response rather than a list of sources.

When teaching students about these differences, it's helpful to model a generative AI tool alongside another online tool they use often. Show students how a search engine delivers a list of links based on keyword matching, while a generative model creates original content in direct response to a user's request. From there, invite students to explore the capabilities of each—highlighting how generative tools allow for interaction, revision, and real-time shaping of output. These experiences help students build awareness of how different technologies respond to their input and when to choose one tool over another. Understanding this distinction lays the foundation for using generative AI models effectively and becoming a more strategic, flexible, and independent learner in today's digital world.

Common Classroom Applications

Elementary Examples

- **Compare search engines and generative AI results.** Guide students to compare a search engine and a generative model by asking the same question in both. After reviewing the results, ask students to notice: What did the search engine give me? What did the AI generate? Use this as an entry point to explain how one retrieves and the other creates based on patterns.

- **Turn the class into a "generator."** No technology needed! Show students how AI generates content by assembling information from a variety of sources. Challenge the class with an initial story starter like, "Once upon a time . . . " and have one student complete the statement. Now offer a second prompt based on the student's response. "But then the dragon said . . . " and have a second student complete the sentence. Keep the story going until everyone has completed a prompt and discuss how the final story was built using all their ideas.

- **The training set game.** Explain that generative AI is trained on data, and that a dataset comprised only of cats will not recognize a dog. Use Teachable Machine by Google to show examples of how datasets influence what a model knows.

Secondary Examples

- **Build an AI vocabulary.** Teach foundational vocabulary in generative AI like *datasets*, *models*, *tokens*, and *prediction* using slides or short videos. Have students use these in writing about generative AI, creating metaphors or analogies (e.g., "Datasets are like ingredients in a chili recipe because they come from every aisle in the grocery store.").

- **Create a "From Input to Output" flowchart.** Use generative AI vocabulary to create a flowchart of the actions: training data [arrow] model [arrow] token [arrow] prediction [arrow]. Students can then create a series of comic strip panels to illustrate how the sequence works.

- **Train your own dataset.** Older students can use Teachable Machine, a free platform from Google, to build their own model using data they have generated. For instance, they can train a model using soccer kicking and passing techniques, musical sounds on a harmonica, or to make their own facial recognition tool.

Strategy in Action

Teach students how the generative AI got there in the first place through reverse-engineering. Present a range of AI-generated outputs, such as short paragraphs, images, poems, or data visualizations, without seeing the prompts that produced them. Their task is to work backward: to reverse engineer the original input or identify the likely features of the training data that could have led to the output. Students then discuss and write their hypotheses, drawing on their understanding of how generative AI uses patterns in training data to predict and generate outputs. The purpose is to demystify the "magic" behind generative AI by helping students see it as a predictive, pattern-based tool rather than an intelligent thinker.

To scaffold the activity, the teacher can begin with modeling, walking through one example with the class using a think-aloud strategy. Next, students can work in small groups with a selection of AI outputs (text or image) that vary in accuracy, style, or perspective. Each group is given a chart or slide to fill out:

1. Describe the output.
2. Infer the likely prompt or source data.
3. Explain why the AI might have made certain choices.

For higher-level analysis, students can be asked to identify whether the output might reflect bias, missing information, or a lack of context.

Teacher Moves

- Ask students, "How do you believe this author/artist/chatbot got this information?" to build the habit and disposition of considering sources.
- Add a similar reflection question to AI-approved tasks.
- Use visuals, shapes, and other non-linguistic examples of patterns, such as tessellations, to link pattern detection to the way generative AI works.

Student Moves

- Listen for students' use of language related to generative AI models and watch for its use in their writing.
- Create "unplugged" non-generative AI experiences by asking students to make predictions using their own knowledge, such as predicting the next letter in a word, the next word in a sentence, or the next section in a reading, then discuss how generative AI systems make predictions based on pattern recognition.
- Use a single topic to generate at least three different types of content. This exercise highlights the different types of formats that the generative models can produce (lists, paragraphs, poems, songs, or even a list of questions and answers).

> **Extension or Adaptation Idea**
>
> - **Advanced learners:** Challenge students to change the style, tone, or word choice in prompts using different generative AI platforms and compare the output results. Ask them to form explanations for why these variances occur.
> - **Multilingual learners:** Ask students to explore generative AI models in other languages and draw conclusions about how linguistic and cultural elements may influence how a platform performs.
> - **Emerging readers:** Use MapSkip, a free app, to generate stories using Google Maps. This allows young children to use familiar locations in their own community to develop a digital story. This introduces students to a large dataset (Google Maps) to create original stories.
> - **Cross-content:** Introduce computational thinking, which is a process used in generative AI, to the classroom. Students can break a code in mathematics and draw character connections in English, then compare how these two examples of computational thinking are alike in terms of pattern detection.

Skill Progression by Grade Band

Grade Band	Skills	Supports
K–2: Curious Creators	• Understand that AI can make pictures, poems, or stories • Notice that AI creations can be surprising or a little strange • Begin to talk about how AI "mixes ideas" to create what users want	• Selection of AI-generated and student-created stories or images • **Human made, AI made, or too tricky to tell sort activity** • Sentence stems like "This sounds made up because . . . "
3–5: Prompt and Play Explorers	• Explain the difference between generating and retrieving • Try different prompts and compare what changes and what stays the same • Begin to reflect on how the AI didn't "know" what to make, but rather that it predicted based on patterns	• Prompt remix station using variations of the same input • **Activity for matching common AI metaphors (blender, parrot, mirror) to examples of output** • Reflection frames like "I was surprised that AI . . . " or "I noticed that ___ was created because ___."
6–8: Prompt-to-Product Thinkers	• Describe how AI uses training data to generate new responses • Evaluate outputs for originality, usefulness, or weirdness • Reflect on what may have shaped the AI's response	• **Chart of common add-on prompts to use after initial input** • Training data prediction chart to help students infer where AI might have learned certain ideas or phrases

GENERATIVE MODELS

Grade Band	Skills	Supports
9–12: Generation Analysts	• Analyze how generative AI recombines data to create something new and how changing just one aspect of a prompt generates entirely different content • Evaluate strengths and limits of generative models for different purposes	• Comparison task labeling AI-created vs. human-sourced elements • Case study analysis on helpful and misleading generative outputs • **Curated AI-generated samples around one topic from varying platforms to support analysis and discussion**

 Examples of the boldface supports above can be found on the book's companion website here: https://companion.corwin.com/courses/TeachingStudentsAI

Personalized Mastery-Based Learning

WHAT IS IT?

Personalized learning with AI refers to the use of artificial intelligence to adapt instruction based on each student's needs, pace, and understanding. AI systems analyze how a student learns and provide targeted support, such as hints, practice problems, or feedback. This helps students master concepts more effectively while giving teachers insight into progress and challenges.

WHY IT MATTERS

Personalized mastery-based learning is the foundation of a vision for the future of education, and it builds on the work of educational psychologist Benjamin Bloom (1984). Bloom introduced the concept of mastery learning, arguing that with enough time and proper instruction, nearly all students could achieve a high level of understanding. This landmark study on mastery learning further showed that one-on-one tutoring can improve student performance by two standard deviations over traditional classroom instruction. This challenged the traditional model where time is fixed and learning varies, often leaving students behind. In most classrooms today, students are expected to move through content at the same pace, even if they have not fully understood the material. This creates learning gaps that grow over time, especially in subjects like math where each concept builds on the one before it. Mastery-based learning reverses this pattern by allowing students to move forward only when they have demonstrated strong understanding.

Artificial intelligence in education can support this model by analyzing student responses and adjusting instruction to match their needs. With timely feedback, extra practice, and personalized support, students are more likely to stay in the optimal zone for learning, gaining confidence and deeper understanding as they progress at a pace that works for them.

HOW IT WORKS

Human-like Socratic learning combines the power of guided questioning with the personalized responsiveness of a skilled tutor. Rooted in the Socratic method, this approach emphasizes asking thoughtful, open-ended questions that prompt students to examine their thinking, articulate reasoning, and deepen understanding. This is especially true when tutoring involves dialogue-rich, scaffolded questioning rather than simple answer-giving. Educational research supports the effectiveness of this approach in developing metacognition, critical thinking, and durable learning. Dozens of studies have revealed that intelligent tutoring systems (ITSs) can impact educational outcomes, especially in terms of significantly improved student attitudes toward learning and test scores (Huang et al., 2025). Importantly, they should supplement, not replace, traditional instruction. For optimal use, educators must consider the design, fit with curriculum, and student needs.

What makes AI-based Socratic tools like Khanmigo promising is their ability to replicate some of the most effective aspects of human tutoring at scale. By asking questions that guide student thinking, offering just-in-time feedback, and adapting to individual responses, these AI systems can create a more personalized and cognitively engaging learning experience, one that closely mirrors what effective human tutors do.

> ## Common Classroom Applications
>
> ### Elementary Examples
>
> - **"My learning profile" book.** Students create a simple booklet with pages about their favorite subjects, their interests, and their goals for learning. Guide students to reflect on how they learn best and what helps them stay motivated.
>
> - **Learning playlist.** Students build a "playlist" of learning activities they enjoy, such as videos, books, practice games, and hands-on projects. Some adaptive learning platforms have built-in tools to do so. This encourages choice and decision-making and helps them recognize the value of working at their own pace.
>
> - **Weekly reflection note catchers.** Build metacognition and self-directed learning skills by having students write or draw what they learned, what was hard, and what helped them. This can help them see learning as a personal journey, not just a set of tasks.
>
> ### Secondary Examples
>
> - **"What works for me" infographics.** Rather than conventional all-about-me beginning of the year activities, invite students to develop an infographic of ways they learn best, distractions to avoid, and how they tackle challenges. Students can then record themselves in short introductions for placement on the class's learning management system.
>
> - **Learner identity interviews.** Students interview, and are interviewed by, peers about their learning habits, strengths, and challenges, then summarize findings in a joint podcast. This peer-to-peer activity can promote a positive classroom climate and give students new ideas for strategies they might try themselves. These can be assigned throughout the first quarter of the school year so that the podcasts are spaced.
>
> - **Build personalized learning plans.** At the beginning of every instructional unit, review the unit success criteria. Next, have students rank order the success criteria from easiest to hardest, then make a plan for how they will personalize their mastery learning using AI and human resources to achieve these goals (Fisher et al., 2023).

Strategy in Action

Many students are unaware of how they learn, thinking that somehow it just happens, or, when they struggle, believing that others are somehow more intelligent than they are. Their unawareness about learning can put them at a disadvantage when it comes to personalizing their learning. Cognitive strategy stations are a hands-on classroom activity designed to introduce students to research-backed learning strategies that enhance memory, understanding, and retention. This activity draws on findings from cognitive science and neuroscience to help students explore what actually supports effective learning.

The class is divided into four stations, each centered on a different evidence-based strategy: retrieval practice, spaced repetition, dual coding, and elaboration.

- At the *retrieval practice station*, students close their notes and attempt to recall information from a previous lesson, experiencing how effortful recall strengthens memory.

- At the *spaced repetition station*, they compare their recall of concepts studied yesterday versus a week ago, helping them notice the benefits of spacing learning over time.

- In the *dual coding station*, students convert text into visuals or interpret visuals into words, reinforcing how combining words and images improves comprehension.

- At the *elaboration station*, they answer *how* and *why* questions about a concept and connect it to other concepts, deepening their understanding through explanation while promoting transfer learning.

After rotating through each station, students reflect on which strategies felt most natural or effective and consider how they might use it to personalize their own mastery learning. It can help students begin to personalize their learning journeys using tools grounded in research, rather than on myths or misconceptions.

Teacher Moves

- Say, "You can take more time on this concept. What matters is that you understand it, not how fast you finish."

- Provide flexible pacing options and allow students to revisit assessments or tasks after additional practice.

- Use formative checks to guide feedback and conference with students about their progress and next steps and ask how AI can play a role in their goals.

Student Moves

- Ask for feedback. Promote routines that require students to make requests for feedback on a specific part of their work rather than asking, "Is this right?"

- Track their own progress. Provide tools for students to track their own progress toward mastery using charts, logs, or digital dashboards.

- Select different paths for support from choices you provide, including videos, small group reteaching, and AI prompts they can use, based on their needs.

Extension or Adaptation Idea

- **Advanced learners:** Invite students to use AI tools to generate their own learning pathway for a unit, including self-selected resources, pacing guides, and checkpoints for mastery. Have them develop prompts to teach AI about how they best learn and share their results with others.

- **Multilingual learners:** Encourage students to track their learning progress by using AI to produce visual tools like color-coded charts or illustrated journals, with support for both academic language and content mastery.

- **Emerging readers:** Use AI-powered text-to-speech and image generation tools to help emergent readers access complex content in age-appropriate, engaging formats. Let students give voice prompts to the chatbot to ask questions about a topic and receive simplified, illustrated responses they can explain or retell in their own words to show understanding.

- **Cross-content:** Design cross-disciplinary projects where students use AI to guide their own learning paths based on mastery goals across subjects. For example, a student studying ecosystems in science could use AI to build a customized research plan, receive feedback on a draft of a persuasive essay in ELA, and track math-related data trends from weather reports.

Skill Progression by Grade Band

Grade Band	Skills	Supports
K–2: Becoming a Self-Aware Learner	• Recognize when they need help • Follow simple routines for learning • Express learning preferences • Reflect with prompts ("I learned . . . ")	• Visual schedules and cues • Lesson plans for teacher modeling and think-alouds • **Choice boards for AI support** • Structured peer sharing
3–5: Managing My Learning	• Set short-term learning goals • Track progress with guidance • Use feedback to revise work • Choose from a menu of learning tasks	• **Graphic organizers for goal setting** • Feedback rubrics with student-friendly language • Weekly check-ins • Access to AI tutors or intelligent planning tools
6–8: Owning My Learning Path	• Plan and monitor learning steps • Advocate for resources or support • Use multiple strategies to meet goals • Reflect independently	• Digital learning logs or portfolios • Lessons on using learning strategies • Personalized goal conferences • **Guided reflection template for AI tool explorations**
9–12: Directing My Mastery Journey	• Set long-term and unit-level goals • Evaluate learning products against standards • Adjust pace and path with learning intentions and goals in mind	• **Interactive mastery trackers for AI skill development** • Self-assessment rubrics aligned to standards • Models of plans for student-established deadlines

 Examples of the boldface supports above can be found on the book's companion website here: https://companion.corwin.com/courses/TeachingStudentsAI

Human-in-the-Loop Experiences

WHAT IS IT?

"Human in the loop" refers to the essential role humans play when working with AI by guiding the process, making decisions, and applying personal judgment from the initial prompt to the final output. As we teach students about AI, it's critical to help them become active users who stay in control of their tasks. AI makes suggestions; humans make decisions.

WHY IT MATTERS

A widely used analogy compares AI to riding an electric bike: Just because the bike adds power doesn't mean the rider forgets how to balance, brake, or steer. Those foundational skills still matter. Another helpful analogy is using GPS while driving. It's useful, even essential at times, but not foolproof. Drivers still need to pay attention, make decisions, and know when to trust their own judgment. AI works the same way: It can guide the process, but students must stay in the driver's seat. Similarly, AI should serve as a boost, but not a replacement for critical thinking. Students need to see AI as an augmentation tool and recognize that the real power lies not in humans or AI alone, but in humans and AI working together (Drake, 2023).

HOW IT WORKS

AI is powerful and persuasive and is designed to respond to almost any request; it can often appear superhuman. But without guidance, students may treat AI as the expert and give it the final say. That's why teaching students to "stay in the loop" by questioning, editing, and refining AI output is essential. Highlighting and teaching this idea protects original thinking, deepens understanding, and reinforces human insight. As Holmes and colleagues (2019) note, students need to learn how to work *with* AI through reflection and critique, not rely on it passively. Ding and colleagues (2023) reported that anthropomorphism, which is the belief that an object or an animal possesses human characteristics, can lead students to believe that the chatbot is a person. In particular, they noted that students in their study subscribed warmth and competence in their belief that AI could solve any problem they posed.

When teaching about AI, lead by emphasizing that the human, not the technology, is in charge. Teaching students to be mindful of the H-T-H (Human–Technology–Human) formula helps them understand that technology, including generative AI, is not an end in itself but rather is a tool that connects human input to human needs. AI has the potential to revolutionize how learning can occur in the classroom, especially in its potential to personalize learning, serve as a "super-tutor," and work as a teaching assistant (Khan, 2024). This mindset encourages students to think critically about how they design prompts (the human director), how AI systems process and generate responses (the technology), and how they or others interpret and act on those responses (the human analyzer). By emphasizing this cycle, students learn to see themselves as active participants in the process, responsible for both the quality of the input and the ethical evaluation of the output. It fosters agency, accountability, and thoughtful use of AI in learning and everyday life.

Common Classroom Applications

Elementary Examples

- **Create "I Decide What I Learn Next" checkpoints.** After using an AI tool to suggest next steps in their learning path (e.g., which skill to practice), students pause and evaluate: Do I agree? What do I know about myself that the AI might not? This reinforces principles of metacognition and self-direction within AI-supported environments.

- **Use tutoring transparency logs.** Students keep a simple log when working with AI tutors: what they asked, what they received, what they accepted, and what they changed or ignored. The goal is to promote mindful use and help students track when and why human judgment overrules AI.

- **Role-play "When to Ask a Human" situations.** Build the disposition that humans stay essential in complex moments. Students role-play scenarios where an AI tutor gives incomplete, confusing, or overly generic feedback. They must decide: Is this the moment to bring in a teacher, peer, or expert?

Secondary Examples

- **Design your ideal learning coach.** Learning works best when both human and AI strengths are balanced. Have students design their ideal learning coach using a blend of AI and human features. What should the chatbot do, such as tracking progress and providing hints, and what humans should do to encourage, listen, and adapt.

- **Provide decision logs for AI-enhanced learning.** These are ideal to embed in AI-supported tutoring sessions and adaptive learning platforms, as well as content review study sessions. Ask students to document decisions made, especially what they accepted, modified, or rejected from the chatbot's suggestions.

- **Design a human-AI partnership plan.** Encourage digital ethics and critical thinking by having students work in groups to design an ideal system for their class, where AI helps personalize learning, but human support is still central. They must assign roles to AI and humans and explain their choices.

Strategy in Action

Help students see that using AI doesn't mean turning off their brains; it requires that they turn them on. Show students how to stay "in the loop" by reviewing and revising AI-generated content with a critical eye. For example, in a lesson on opinion writing, challenge students to consider whether people have the right to be forgotten online. After brainstorming and drafting independently, students enter their own claim and reasons into an AI platform and ask for additional suggestions, such as additional reasons, supporting details, or possible counterarguments. Provide some guiding questions to foster verification and analysis:

- What parts of this match what I was trying to say?
- What ideas might distract from my point?
- Does anything here contradict or weaken my claim?
- How would I rewrite this in my own words?
- Can I revise my response using any of this content?

While the teacher demonstrates this digitally, students can practice the same process on printed copies by marking up the AI output and making revisions based on their goals. Although this may not reflect how students will use AI in the long term, the printed version made the human-in-the-loop process visible. It serves as both a learning tool and a formative check, reinforcing that while AI can assist, the human stays in control.

Teacher Moves

- Say, "What do you know that the AI doesn't?"
- Provide examples where human judgment improved or corrected AI outputs. "The AI gave us a starting point, but now it's our job to think critically."

Student Moves

- Pause to consider, "Is this something a teacher or classmate would say too?"
- Reflect in writing, "I accepted this part of the AI's response, but changed this part because . . . "
- Seek a second opinion from a human when the AI answer feels unclear or incomplete.
- Annotate AI output to show where human insight is needed.

Extension or Adaptation Idea

- **Advanced learners:** Challenge students to evaluate and redesign an AI learning interaction (e.g., a chatbot conversation or math problem feedback) by identifying where human input and oversight were weak or missing and propose improvements.

- **Multilingual learners:** Have students use a translation AI (like DeepL or Google Translate) to translate a text between languages, then work in pairs to revise the output based on their cultural and linguistic knowledge.

- **Emerging readers:** Students use a text-to-speech AI tool to hear a simple sentence, then decide whether the voice said the sentence with the correct emotion or meaning, and revise the sentence if needed, giving them control over how AI outputs are interpreted and adjusted for clarity and intent.

- **Cross-content:** In a science and ELA crossover, students use AI to summarize scientific data, then work in writing teams to clarify the summary and make it more understandable for a younger audience. Emphasize that AI can handle patterns and structure, but humans refine language, purpose, and audience awareness.

Skill Progression by Grade Band

Grade Band	Skills	Supports
K–2: Foundations of Feedback and Storytelling	• Recognize that AI gives answers, but people ask questions • Notice when something sounds "off" or confusing and talk about it • Explain how a person helped them think, not just the computer	• Role-play scenarios: "Who said it—me or the machine?" • **Task cards to sort: What people do, what AI can do, what humans and AI can do** • Sentence starters: "I think that because . . . " and "A person would know . . . "
3–5: Beginning to Revise With AI Support	• Compare how an AI response is different from a friend's or teacher's response • Reflect on what's missing when only AI is used • Begin to explain why people still matter, even when AI can help	• Sample AI vs. human responses to explore together • **Tool for deciding when to ask a person vs. AI** • Reflection starters: "AI gave me ____, but my partner helped me ____."
6–8: Purposeful Revision and Feedback Cycles	• Use AI to brainstorm or give feedback, then revise based on peer ideas • Judge when AI helps and when it doesn't • Explain how human thinking shaped their final work	• Peer review forms that include "What did AI help with?" • **Decision pathways that help students decide when to use AI, ask a peer, or rely on their own thinking** • Tools for tracking AI feedback vs. teacher or peer feedback

Grade Band	Skills	Supports
9–12: Strategic Revision, Reflection, and Transfer	• Critically analyze the limits of AI and the importance of human voice • Make intentional choices about how, when, and why to use AI • Reflect on where their final thinking shows independent or collaborative insight	• **Self-assessment rubrics that include human-in-the-loop checkpoints** • Case studies that show ethical or creative missteps without human input • Protocols for tracking changes from AI prompt to final product

 Examples of the boldface supports above can be found on the book's companion website here: https://companion.corwin.com/courses/TeachingStudentsAI

Collective Intelligence

WHAT IS IT?

Collective intelligence is the shared intelligence of a group of people. In the context of AI, it refers to the interfacing of humans and technology to lead to a deeper range of insights and solutions.

Collective intelligence is the idea that when humans and AI work together—each bringing different strengths—they can produce better thinking, stronger work, and deeper insight than either could achieve alone. In school settings, this often looks like a student collaborating with an AI platform to brainstorm, revise, organize, or refine their thinking. Unlike using technology to do the work for you or arrive at a single answer, collective intelligence is an ongoing, interactive process, or a human-AI collaboration that unfolds through thoughtful engagement. The user doesn't just type a prompt and move on; they return to the tool, ask better questions, compare outputs, and make decisions about what to keep, change, or reject. It's an active process, not a passive one.

WHY IT MATTERS

Unlike the idea of keeping the human in the loop, which focuses on oversight and control by making sure a person supervises or approves AI use, collective intelligence shifts the focus to active participation. It's not just about watching or reviewing what AI produces. It's about working with the AI to shape, refine, and evolve the thinking. It's like a group project where both contributors, the human user and the AI platform, bring something valuable. The student brings voice, context, values, and intent. The AI brings speed, suggestions, structure, and synthesis. Both contribute to the final outcome and have a role in maintaining the quality of the work. And that is exactly the point. We want to make sure that student thinking isn't reduced to solitary interactions between a single learner and a chatbot. Students must also have lots of experiences with working alongside classmates, while leveraging AI to deepen the group's knowledge. AI is not at its most powerful when it does the work for you. It is most powerful when it helps you, and the group, to think better. That's why it is important for students to learn how to move between their own ideas and what the AI provides. They need to understand that the process is ongoing and collaborative, not one-step or one-sided.

HOW IT WORKS

When student teams work with AI as a thought partner, they engage in a dynamic form of collective intelligence that enhances learning through collaboration, critical thinking, and metacognition. AI tools like ChatGPT or Khanmigo offer real-time feedback, idea generation, and content clarification, but their real value emerges when students interact with these tools together by critiquing responses, refining prompts, and building on AI-generated ideas. This mirrors dialogic learning, where knowledge is co-constructed through conversation and reasoning (Mercer & Howe, 2012). AI becomes an additional "voice" in the group, one that invites students to question, verify, and synthesize, promoting higher-order thinking.

Research on collaborative learning and knowledge-building communities supports the idea that when students learn from each other, especially in response to complex tasks, they develop deeper understanding (Bereiter & Scardamalia, 2014). Adding AI expands the group's capacity to explore diverse perspectives and simulate expert input, helping learners at all levels contribute meaningfully. As students evaluate AI suggestions and integrate them with their own ideas, they practice epistemic agency, which is the ability to take responsibility for what and how they learn (Damşa et al., 2010). Real collaboration between humans and AI depends on more than generating good content. It also depends on how users manage memory, attention, and reasoning across both contributions (Gupta et al., 2025). Students need to keep track of where ideas came from, make sure they are working toward a shared goal, and revise until everything fits together as a seamless whole. Teaching this level of awareness helps students produce stronger final work and builds the thinking habits they'll need as collaboration with AI becomes a regular part of learning and life.

Common Classroom Applications

Elementary Examples

- **The "We Try First" rule.** Before accessing an AI tool, student teams must first attempt the task using their own knowledge, discussion, and resources. Only after agreeing that they've reached a limit (e.g., "We're stuck," "We can't agree," or "We need more info") may they consult the AI, then they reflect: Was the AI helpful? Did it change our thinking?

- **"Think First" station rotations.** Students rotate through task stations (e.g., writing a paragraph, solving a word problem, brainstorming ideas), but before using an AI assistant, they must work as a team to try solving the task together. Only after attempting and discussing it can they visit the "AI Helper Station" to compare answers or seek support.

- **Use partner power checks.** During inquiry or project time, students have laminated charts labeled "Check with a teammate," "Check with AI," or "Check with both." As they work, they slide a clothespin to the option they chose and write or draw a reason on a sticky note. This supports early reflection on the different kinds of knowledge AI and peers provide.

Secondary Examples

- **Use an "AI-as-Advisor" protocol.** Before using AI, groups first brainstorm multiple solutions or perspectives on a challenge (e.g., solving a historical dilemma or writing a persuasive article). Then, they ask AI the same question to compare with their human-generated ideas. They vote as a group: Which ideas feel stronger or more thoughtful and why? This emphasizes critical comparison and the human ability to judge nuance, ethics, and creativity.

(Continued)

(Continued)

- **Set up strategy consultations during project work.** When students tackle a complex task, such as planning a school improvement proposal, it is important for them to cultivate awareness of AI's strengths (information recall) versus the team's strengths (emotional insight, local knowledge). Ask teams to document when they choose to rely on team discussion versus when to query the AI. After major decisions, they note how they leveraged human, collective, and AI intelligence.
- **Assign roles in team projects.** Teams assign formal roles to one another to ensure the project is completed in a timely way. Develop team roles that include AI. For example,
    - Task Manager: keeps the group focused on the goal.
    - Strategy Suggester: proposes how to divide labor among AI, peers, or both.
    - AI Operator: assumes primary responsibility for inputting prompts and sharing the chatbot's responses with the group.
    - Reflector/Recorder: tracks decisions on the strategy consultations and writes justifications.

Strategy in Action

In the Brain + Bot Challenge, students work in teams to solve creative tasks by combining their own thinking with support from an AI assistant. Each group begins by tackling a challenge, such as writing a riddle, inventing a creature, or planning a healthy school lunch, using only their shared ideas. They record their brainstorming under the heading *Our Brainstorm*, focusing on what they know and how they can build on each other's thinking. Once they've made a strong attempt, teams prepare a clear, focused question to ask an AI tool. The AI response is recorded under *What the Bot Said*, and students then compare, critique, and combine ideas from both sources. Together, they create a final product labeled *Made by Brain + Bot*, choosing what to keep from each contributor. Finally, students reflect on what they did best as a team and when AI was helpful.

Teacher Moves

- Ask teams, "What does your group already know that might help solve this?"
- When facilitating a group that is stuck, ask, "How could combining your ideas make the answer stronger?"
- Facilitate whole-class share-outs that highlight how teams learned from each other.

Student Moves

- Provide accountable talk sentence stems (Michaels et al., 2008) that facilitate group consensus and decision-making:
  - "Do we all agree on what we're doing?"
  - "I like what you said, and I think we can add . . . "
  - "Here's my idea. Tell me if it makes sense."
- Have "share the air" pauses to ensure that quieter voices, as well as AI, are invited into the conversation, e.g., "We haven't heard from you, yet. What are you thinking about right now?"
- Provide prompt frames that teams can use to improve their queries.

Extension or Adaptation Idea

- **Advanced learners:** Teams explore a complex, open-ended issue (e.g., reducing screen time) by dividing into subgroups with differing perspectives. After each side presents, the group consults an AI tool to generate a neutral synthesis of both perspectives. Students then evaluate the AI's synthesis, challenge or revise it using their own insights, and produce a final team-authored version.
- **Multilingual learners:** Students work in multilingual teams to co-construct solutions or ideas using scaffolds as needed (e.g., bilingual glossaries, sentence frames, translated prompts). One student contributes in their home language or preferred mode, and teammates paraphrase or build on it.
- **Emerging readers:** Students use an AI captioning tool of visuals (with guidance). Then, in small groups, they discuss what the AI got right in the image and what needs adjustment, using oral language and peer input. The team revises their idea or drawing and captions it themselves, making AI a visual thought partner rather than a source of finished work.
- **Cross-content:** In an interdisciplinary project, such as designing a playground, each group member contributes from a subject lens: math for measurements, science for materials, art for layout, and ELA for explanation. At key checkpoints, students ask AI for suggestions or feedback (e.g., "What are eco-friendly building materials?"), but they must vote on whether to use, modify, or reject the chatbot's suggestions.

Skill Progression by Grade Band

Grade Band	Skills	Supports
K–2: Learning to Think Together	• Take turns speaking and listening • Share ideas and respond to others • Recognize when to ask for help • Begin using group tools (charts, visuals)	• Visual turn-taking cues • **Sentence stems for sharing and building ideas with others** • Group roles with visuals
3–5: Building Ideas as a Team	• Add on to others' ideas • Ask clarifying questions • Use shared tools like charts or organizers • Begin making group decisions (e.g., who asks AI?)	• Group thinking routines (e.g., Think-Pair-Square) • "Try It and Tweak It" activity focused on making changes to AI content • **Graphic organizer for building a better idea with AI support** • Reflection sheets for group choices
6–8: Collaborating Strategically	• Assign roles and manage group tasks • Decide when to use AI vs. peer thinking • Synthesize multiple perspectives • Reflect on team strengths and decisions	• Protocols for using AI in group work • **Role cards for group use of AI (AI Manager, Synthesizer, Clarifier, Checker, Note Catcher, and Connector)** • Group decision logs or digital collaboration boards • Teacher check-ins to mediate and coach
9–12: Leading Collective Intelligence	• Facilitate group discussions and debates • Critique and refine peer and AI-generated ideas • Distribute tasks strategically across humans and tools • Evaluate group process and adapt strategies	• AI ethics and critique frameworks • Collaborative project planning tools (e.g., Trello, Google Workspace, NotebookLM) • **Prompt maps with revision notes** • Self-check tool: "Is this still my thinking?" with indicators for voice, clarity, and intent

 Examples of the boldface supports above can be found on the book's companion website here: https://companion.corwin.com/courses/TeachingStudentsAI

Adaptive Platforms

WHAT IS IT?

Adaptive platforms are AI-powered tools that personalize learning by adjusting content, pace of learning, or supports based on a student's performance or behavior. These tools are designed to meet learners where they are and provide a path that matches their need.

WHY IT MATTERS

Chances are very good that your students are already using AI, whether you (and they) realize it or not. Tools like Khanmigo, iReady, DreamBox, and even Duolingo are all AI-powered adaptive platforms. They are designed to observe how students interact with content and then shape what comes next.

Since adaptive platforms shape learning paths, they influence what students learn next, the kinds of support they receive, and even how long they stay on a topic. That's why it's important for students to understand that these platforms respond to *their* behavior. If students rush through questions, click randomly, or don't engage thoughtfully, the platform may adjust in ways that don't support their growth. On the other hand, when students take their time, show what they really know, and ask for support when needed, the platform is more likely to offer the right kind of challenge or reinforcement. In this way, students aren't just using adaptive platforms. They're helping shape what the platform does next.

This kind of personalization isn't limited to education, making it all the more important to teach as we prepare students for what is to come. Platforms like TikTok, YouTube, and Spotify also track user behavior and adjust what they recommend next. Recognizing that both entertainment and education platforms use similar adaptive approaches can help students become more thoughtful and critical consumers and users of AI-generated content both in and out of the classroom. The goal isn't to reject these tools, but to use them more intentionally and with greater awareness.

HOW IT WORKS

Adaptive platforms are always collecting information. As students interact with a task, whether completing problems, reading a passage, answering questions, or clicking through lessons, the system gathers data about their responses. These data fuel what comes next. Most platforms operate using an if-then logic algorithm. *If* a student gets several questions right in a row, *then* the platform might offer something more challenging. *If* a student struggles on a particular type of problem, *then* the system might offer more practice or adjust the level of support. This kind of real-time adjustment is what makes the platform feel personalized, but it also means the experience is constantly being shaped by the student's choices. Studies on these intelligent tutoring systems (the more formal term) show that they are responsive to students with a variety of learning profiles because of their ability to personalize learning (Chien-Chang et al., 2023). The learner profile system is especially important. These systems use student responses to learn more about the student. For example, users are asked about interests, strengths, learning goals, and other learner attributes. A systematic review of studies on these self-declared profiles found that they can impact the learning path (Mejeh & Rehm, 2024).

> ### Common Classroom Applications
>
> **Elementary Examples**
>
> - **Make the if-then logic visible.** After students complete a set of questions in an adaptive learning platform, pause and ask, "What do you think the platform noticed?" or "Why do you think it gave you this next?" This encourages early pattern recognition and helps students reflect on how their actions affect what comes next.
>
> - **Introduce platform reflection routines.** Use simple sentence starters like, "The platform helped me because . . . " or "Next time I want it to show me more about. . . . " Have students complete these reflections after each adaptive task to build habits of metacognition and ownership.
>
> - **Use comparison activities.** Let students experience a fixed learning task (printed worksheet, class assessment, or shared video link) and then compare it with an adaptive one. Prompt discussion around questions like, "How did the computer know what to give me next?" or "Which one felt more helpful and why?"
>
> **Secondary Examples**
>
> - **Prompt reflection on the learning path.** After working in a skill-based reading tool, ask students to annotate their learning pathway: "Where did it shift? What did I do that caused the change? Did it help?" This builds awareness that the system is reactive to their performance.
>
> - **Connect to everyday apps.** Invite students to compare their experience in adaptive learning tools to recommendation systems on TikTok, YouTube, or Spotify. Ask them, "How are these tools similar? What do they learn from you? How do you stay in control of what's shown next?" Use this as a bridge between in- and out-of-school AI awareness.
>
> - **Predict the path before using the platform.** Before logging into a familiar adaptive tool, ask students to write or sketch what they think the learning path will be based on their current understanding. After using the platform, have them compare their prediction to what actually happened.

Strategy in Action

To help students understand how adaptive platforms respond to user input, create a short inquiry-based activity that invites students to reverse-engineer the learning path generated by an AI-powered tool. After completing a session on an adaptive platform that students are already familiar with, ask them to work in pairs or small groups to map what they believed the system noticed about them, what they got right or wrong, how quickly they moved, and what kinds of tasks they were shown.

Next, ask students to develop a simple if-then chart based on their experiences, for example,

If I got the fraction question wrong, then it gave me a review video.

If I finished early, then it moved me ahead.

Students share and compare their charts with peers who had taken different paths. This can start an authentic and meaningful conversation about how AI-powered platforms adjust based on performance and behavior and help students recognize that what they see is personalized, not random.

Teacher Moves

- Check alignment with existing data and consider how well this matches what you already know from classroom assessments and observations.

- Before students begin, explain that the platform adjusts to their progress and set the purpose for this adaptive time, emphasizing that their effort shapes the experience.

- Facilitate comparison conversations and guide students in how to compare how the platform adapted for each of them, not only in terms of difficulty, but in the type of support provided.

- Highlight how AI responds differently based on what each student needs in the moment.

Student Moves

- Ask students to pause before beginning to consider what skill the platform is focusing on and why it might it have chosen that.

- After the session, ask students to compare experiences with a peer.

- Ask questions when the path doesn't make sense. If they're unsure why the platform gave them a certain question, task, or level of support, have them notify you.

> ### Extension or Adaptation Idea
>
> - **Advanced learners:** Act like a platform designer. Pick a subject you know well and create an if-then logic path to guide another student through it. This builds understanding of how adaptive tools respond to different needs and will even help students review content learned.
>
> - **Multilingual learners:** Use visual cards (icons for correct/incorrect, slow/fast, easy/hard) to help provide students with language that helps them reflect on adaptive experiences.
>
> - **Emerging readers:** Work with sentence starters and teacher-created prompts to build simple cause/effect charts based on their activity: "I got it right → it gave me something harder."
>
> - **Cross-content:** Teach about adaptive platforms in other areas, such as those used for drivers' education, aviation training, and world language learning.

Skill Progression by Grade Band

Grade Band	Skills	Supports
K–2: Learning Tool Explorers	• Recognize that learning apps respond to their answers and clicks • Begin to notice when a game or app gets easier or harder • Talk about how their effort affects what happens next	• Whole-class model of an adaptive tool with teacher think-aloud • "What changed?" guided discussion after using a learning app • **"Learning Together With Technology" anchor chart**
3–5: Responsive Learners	• Describe how adaptive platforms adjust based on their choices and pace • Reflect on times when the tool was helpful—or not quite right • Begin to connect thoughtful engagement to better support	• Exit slips: "How did the platform respond to me today?" • **Reflection chart: "Did the lesson feel too easy, too hard, or just right?"** • Simple checklist: "Did I try my best or rush through?"
6–8: Pattern-Aware Users	• Explain how platforms use if-then logic to adapt content • Identify when their actions may have affected the tool's response • Reflect on whether the feedback or path matched their actual need	• **Organizer for students: "What I did/What the platform did next"** • Small group discussion prompts: "Did this match what I needed?" • Teacher-facilitated prompt: "What advice would you give someone using this tool well?"

Grade Band	Skills	Supports
9–12: Intentional Decision-Makers	• Analyze how adaptive platforms influence learning pace and path • Reflect on how their data shapes recommendations and supports • Make intentional choices when using adaptive tools to meet personal learning goals	• **"What I did and what the platform did next" tracking tool** • Journal prompt: "What did this tool assume about me and was it right?" • Peer discussion or portfolio check-in: "How can I take charge of what happens next?"

 Examples of the boldface supports above can be found on the book's companion website here: https://companion.corwin.com/courses/TeachingStudentsAI

AI, Data, and You

WHAT IS IT?

AI tools learn from your behavior. What you click, watch, and type helps personalize your experience and prioritize the AI-fueled interactions you experience. When used for learning, AI's ability to "learn about you" can make the experience feel more targeted, relevant, and helpful. However, it also means these systems are collecting data about you, which has implications for both teacher and student privacy.

WHY IT MATTERS

Today's students grow up in a world where personalization feels normal. From their perspectives, they see learning platforms adjusting lessons and learning pathways, apps recommending content, and ads that seem to "know" exactly what you want. Behind every personalized experience is a system collecting, sorting, and acting on the data users share. Understanding how this data collection and personalization process works is crucial for making informed and protective choices regarding privacy. That understanding can also lead to asking better questions and making smart choices about tool usage. Digital responsibility and added control over their learning and their online lives are essential.

HOW IT WORKS

Helping students understand AI and privacy starts with pulling back the curtain: How is data collected? Who uses it? And what does it mean when a platform "learns" from what you do online? Building agency is the goal. When students start to pause and ask, "Why am I seeing this?" or "Who benefits from knowing this about me?" they begin to think more critically about the systems around them. AI can support this by showing patterns in their own digital behavior, simulating privacy decisions, or helping break down complex tech-speak into plain language.

Research supports the effectiveness of these practices. Students learn best when privacy education is scaffolded. That means connecting their digital actions to real consequences with tools they already use (Leung et al., 2021). Reflecting on how adaptive systems respond to their data can also build self-regulation and decision-making skills that will serve them in school and their future workplaces (Anthonysamy, 2021; Livingstone et al., 2019).

Common Classroom Applications

Elementary Examples

- **Ask, "Who sees me?"** Guide students through a sort-and-discuss activity where they consider what happens when they watch a video, play a game, or log in to a class app. Have them categorize each action based on who might see the data: just them, their teacher, or the company behind the tool. Use this to prompt questions like, "Why do they want to know that?"

- **Play a "What's Private?" sorting game.** Lead lessons and conversations about the types of data that are okay to share and the types of data that should be kept private. Have students sort examples, such as favorite food, hobbies, grades, passwords, address, or middle name, into "Okay to Share" and "Keep Private" categories, and then discuss why some information is more sensitive and shouldn't be shared freely.

- **Introduce a password power challenge.** Teach the importance of strong, private passwords through a friendly classroom competition to build the strongest password using rules (e.g., no names, include numbers and symbols). Let students test weak versus strong passwords with an AI simulator or interactive quiz. Purpose: Introduces safe password creation and why passwords protect personal data.

Secondary Examples

- **Plan an "Accept or Ask" activity.** Students walk through mock pop-ups about data collection. Ask them to vote on whether they would click "accept all" or "ask app not to track," then guide a conversation about what each choice means and how it affects who sees their information.

- **Conduct a digital footprint walk.** Ask students to reflect on their own digital footprint by making a timeline of their typical online activity over a 24-hour period, such as using search engines, opening apps, or posting on social media. Then have them annotate which actions likely involved sharing data and with whom. Use this as a prompt for reflection: "Which of these moments shared the most about you and did you realize it at the time?"

- **Review school district and state guidelines on digital privacy for minors with students.** Many states and provinces have policy guidelines to protect student data use by technology providers. For instance, California has regulations that safeguard student data from misuse by educational technology companies and ensure a safe online learning environment, such as the Student Online Personal Information Protection Act (SOPIPA). Have students investigate protections in their region and compare to the guidelines in other states.

Strategy in Action

To help students build awareness of how AI tools and platforms use personal information, teach students to pause anytime they are asked to enter data, such as their name, birthday, location, or email, and think carefully about what was being requested. The goal isn't to avoid sharing altogether, but to build the habit of asking, "Why does this platform need this information? What might it do with it? Who else might see or use it?"

Students discuss how, in some cases, sharing information could improve the user experience. For example, entering your age might help an AI-powered site adjust reading level or content. But they also learn that some requests might be unnecessary. Help students understand that being a responsible user means thinking critically before clicking "accept," "allow," or "submit," and knowing that they can ask questions before handing over their information.

Teacher Moves

- Introduce key vocabulary like *personal information* and *data privacy* using authentic examples that students already encounter online and in the classroom.

- Create and reference an anchor chart or set of reflection questions like, "Do I know who's asking?" or "Is this safe to share?"

- Embed short check-ins during technology use to prompt student thinking and normalize pausing before sharing data.

Student Moves

- Practice a routine of "pause before you share" when deciding what information to enter into a website, app, or tool.

- Explain their thinking aloud or with a partner when deciding if a piece of information is safe or necessary to share.

- Refer to a classroom chart or set of guiding questions when they are asked for information online, especially names, birthdays, emails, or location.

- Recognize when something feels like too much information and know to ask a trusted adult for help before continuing.

Extension or Adaptation Idea

- **Advanced learners:** Analyze the sign-up process for different tools or platforms and compare what types of data they ask for and why. Then create a set of "green/yellow/red flag" indicators to guide peer use.

- **Multilingual learners:** Invite students to role-play common online scenarios, such as signing into a game or filling out a form, using sentence frames to explain what they would or wouldn't share and why.
- **Emerging readers:** Read picture books like *Chicken Clicking* by Jeanne Willis or *The Technology Tail* by Julia Cook and act out scenarios where characters must decide whether to share information or ask an adult.
- **Cross-content:** In a science unit on data collection, have students compare how scientists gather information, such as weather patterns or animal behavior, to how companies collect personal data online. Discuss any ethical implications that apply.

Skill Progression by Grade Band

Grade Band	Skills	Supports
K–2: Digital Observers	• Recognize that tools remember what they click or choose • Notice when a site or app changes based on past choices • Begin asking, "Why am I seeing this?"	• **"What happens when you click . . . " chart and prompts** • Visuals: "Before I clicked/After I clicked" • Sentence stems: "It changed because I . . . "
3–5: Early Awareness Builders	• Understand that apps collect and use their data to change content • Ask how and why a platform knows what they like • Reflect on how behavior shapes recommendations or feedback	• Interactive scenario cards: "What does the app learn about you?" • T-chart: "What I do/What the platform does next" • **Anchor chart: "Smart clicks vs. risky clicks"**
6–8: Informed Digital Participants	• Explain how digital behavior creates a data trail • Reflect on who might use that data and for what purpose • Ask critical questions about consent, access, and benefit	• Case studies: "Who's tracking what—and why?" • **"Terms of Service" hunt for finding and understanding important information** • Group task: "Would you click accept? Why or why not?"
9–12: Privacy-Conscious Decision-Makers	• Evaluate trade-offs between personalization and privacy • Consider who benefits from their data—and who doesn't • Make informed decisions about what they share, click, or allow	• Reflection prompt: "What data did I give away today—and was it worth it?" • Privacy decision simulations with debriefs • **Structured debate: "Is personalization worth the data cost?"**

 Examples of the boldface supports above can be found on the book's companion website here: https://companion.corwin.com/courses/TeachingStudentsAI

AI Limitations

WHAT IS IT?

AI limitations include not only what a system *can't* do, but also the illusions it creates that make it seem more capable than it is. They are built to deliver complete responses, although not necessarily correct ones. This is at the heart of understanding AI limitations: the boundary between what AI *can* do and what it might *appear* to do.

WHY IT MATTERS

When students don't understand these limitations, they may take AI at face value, accepting everything it produces as accurate, complete, and objective. This overreliance can lead to shallow thinking, repeated errors, or even the spread of misinformation. We should be teaching students to not just accept AI generated content but to question and analyze output. This kind of pause is central to both digital literacy and responsible AI use. It invites students to slow down and consider *why* AI responded the way it did, *how* it generated that answer, and *what* might be missing or misrepresented.

One particularly important limitation we want students to understand is this: No matter how "human-like" an AI system may appear, it is not a person. It's not a real character sharing lived experiences, not a friend checking in on your day, and not a teacher offering advice. In a 2023 study, the Nielsen Norman Group found that a large percentage of AI users assign human traits to AI platforms responding to them as if they had personalities, intentions, or emotions. While adult users may intellectually understand that these systems aren't human, younger users might not draw the same boundary. This makes it especially important to teach students that AI does not truly understand them, care about their well-being, or operate with emotional intent. It may *look* like AI is listening, empathizing, or connecting, but those are illusions created by design, not genuine relationships.

Generative AI is a tool. It can assist, enhance, and even accelerate many tasks but at the end of the day, it does not replace human intelligence. The AI systems we interact with today don't think, feel, or understand. They generate responses based on data patterns, not insight. Teaching students this distinction doesn't limit their use of AI; it strengthens it. When students know where the tool ends and where their thinking begins, they're more equipped to use AI responsibly, creatively, and critically.

HOW IT WORKS

To teach students about AI limitations, it helps to first explain a bit about how these tools are built and how they function. Generative AI systems are trained on massive amounts of data—books, articles, websites, photographs, and more—but the models don't read, analyze, or learn from them in the way humans do. Instead, they identify patterns in the data and use statistical predictions to generate the most likely next word, sentence, or idea based on a user's input (Burtell & Toner, 2024). For example, an analysis of research citations used by freshman college students found that many did not exist, but often contained bits of real information, such as real authors, book titles, or journal names (Watson, 2024).

That's a crucial concept for students to grasp: AI doesn't truly *understand* the information it shares. It doesn't know whether something is true or false, biased or fair, complete or misleading. It can't fact-check itself or draw meaning from personal experience. And because these systems are trained on existing data, which users don't usually see or control, there are built-in risks and limitations, including outdated content, incomplete perspectives, or biased sources. For example, while AI systems like ChatGPT are initially trained on large datasets that reflect information available up to a specific point in time (e.g., at the time of publication the training data for OpenAI's current models was completed in October 2023), they can also access real-time information when connected to available tools. By teaching how generative AI works behind the scenes, educators can help students see why the technology has limits, and why those limits matter. When students understand this, they become better equipped to ask thoughtful questions, evaluate AI responses with a critical lens, and stay in charge of their own learning and thinking.

Common Classroom Applications

Elementary Examples

- **Sounds right, but is it?** Read short AI-generated responses aloud (or display them) and ask students to decide: "Is this definitely true?" "Might this be wrong?" "Should we check another source?" Emphasize that even if something sounds correct, it's important to think and verify.

- **"Fact or fiction" sort.** Share a set of mixed statements (some AI-generated, some human-written, some accurate, some clearly wrong or silly). Have students work in pairs to sort them into "likely true," "needs checking," and "not true," explaining their reasoning and what clues they used.

- **Ask the robot: Can it feel?** Pose prompts to an AI assistant like "How are you feeling today?" or "What's your favorite food?" Then guide a discussion about whether a robot can really have feelings, likes, or experiences. Help students distinguish between *sounding* human and *being* human.

(Continued)

(Continued)

Secondary Examples

- **"Prompt and response" audit.** Have students enter a topical prompt into a chatbot, such as "explain climate change" or "summarize the previous novel we read in English" and then critically evaluate the response. What seems missing? Is the tone overly confident? Are there assumptions, gaps, or inaccuracies? Ask students to annotate or mark up the response and use it to support discussion.

- **Have a gallery walk for AI limitations.** Set up stations with AI-generated outputs that include common limitations (hallucinated facts, biased language, vague generalities, or incorrect math). At each station, students identify the limitation and write how they would revise the response or prompt to address it.

- **Debate the topic: Human or machine?** Students analyze whether a response was written by a human or AI and debate how they could tell. Use this as a springboard to discuss why AI can sound human but lacks actual understanding, emotion, or lived experience, and why that matters when using it to learn, write, or explore ideas.

Strategy in Action

To help students better understand the limitations of AI-generated responses, design a lesson around a prompt connected to students' experiences: "What's the best way to get around our city?" After generating a response using an AI platform, students analyze the output for accuracy, tone, and missing context. Many will quickly notice that the AI might provide generic suggestions that didn't reflect local realities, such as outdated transit info, oversimplified routes, or lack of accessibility considerations. Using their own knowledge and classroom tools, students can annotate the AI response and then revise it to better reflect the needs, experiences, and perspectives of people in their community. The activity helps surface key AI limitations and reinforces the value of human insight and experience in refining and evaluating digital content.

Teacher Moves

- Choose content students have personal experience with to help them more easily spot AI limitations.

- Prepare an AI-generated response that shows subtle issues like vague generalizations, outdated info, or missing perspectives.

- Model critical reading with questions like, "Is this accurate for _____? What's missing? Does this reflect your experience?"

AI LIMITATIONS

Student Moves

- Use critical thinking to evaluate whether particular tasks will pose risks given AI limitations, ensuring using the technology is done with purpose and intention.
- Collaborate in groups to revise or expand the AI response using improved prompts, classroom research, or their own understanding.
- Develop fact-checking protocols for students to verify information.

Extension or Adaptation Idea

- **Advanced learners:** Create a public service announcement (PSA) on one limitation of AI, such as hallucinations, limited knowledge of current events, or inaccurate or incomplete information. Students should use AI tools to create their poster, video, or podcast.
- **Multilingual learners:** Engage students in a conversation about when translation tools are most helpful and when they fall short. Invite them to share personal examples of times when a translation didn't make sense or caused confusion, as well as times when it was genuinely useful. This real-life connection will help them better understand AI limitations.
- **Emerging readers:** Create a simple class-illustrated book called *Why AI Isn't a Person!* Use clear language to explain limitations (e.g., "AI doesn't get jokes," "AI doesn't have feelings"). This might include a section on various tasks (e.g., hugging a friend, writing a poem, solving a puzzle), that are sorted into three categories: Only Humans, Only AI, and Both Humans and AI.
- **Cross-content:** In geography, have students compare AI responses about local systems or landmarks to current events. Use this to show that AI can't replace firsthand knowledge and experiences.

Skill Progression by Grade Band

Grade Band	Skills	Supports
K–2: Early Noticers	• Notice when texts include things that say something odd or feel off • Understand that technology can't think or feel • Talk about why people still need to check answers when using computers	• "Robot or Real?" games using emotional or personal questions • **"What technology can't do" anchor chart**

(Continued)

(Continued)

Grade Band	Skills	Supports
3–5: Growing Skeptics	• Spot when AI leaves out important details • Question how the AI "knows" the content generated • Compare AI answers to what they've learned or experienced	• "Sounds smart, but . . . " activity with confident-but-wrong responses • **"Wait . . . is that right?" error hunt activity** • Anchor chart: "Things AI can't truly understand"
6–8: Developing Critical Users	• Evaluate how AI creates output without understanding • Reflect on tone, accuracy, and missing perspective • Explain how data patterns shape (and limit) responses	• **AI "Confidence vs. Competence" activity with bold but shallow responses** • Group task: Trace an AI mistake back to likely cause (missing context, bad prompt, etc.) • Comparison activity using same prompt with different outputs
9–12: Discerning Decision-Makers	• Analyze how and why AI can mislead or oversimplify • Articulate the risks of accepting AI at face value • Decide when AI output should be trusted, revised, or replaced	• **Case studies of authentic AI mishaps and their impact** • "Truth trap" reflection: What made this output believable but wrong? • Self-audit checklist: "What did I verify? What do I still control?"

 Examples of the boldface supports above can be found on the book's companion website here: https://companion.corwin.com/courses/TeachingStudentsAI

AI and Society

WHAT IS IT?

AI and society is about exploring the ways this technology is shaping industries, influencing culture, raising ethical questions, and affecting everyday life. From social media feeds to facial recognition, from recommendations on streaming platforms to smart assistants like Siri or Alexa, AI plays a growing role in shaping what we see, what we hear, and even what we believe.

WHY IT MATTERS

One of our most important responsibilities as educators is to prepare students for the future, and in doing so, help them build the skills they'll need to make a positive impact, no matter the path they choose. Teaching students about AI and society is a critical part of that work. When we help students understand how AI is shaping the world around them, we give them tools to ask thoughtful questions, notice patterns, evaluate risks, and imagine better possibilities in an AI-driven world. AI is becoming an unavoidable factor in the careers students pursue, the jobs they hold, the communities they live in, and the decisions they face. That's why we want students to be more than just users of AI—we want them to be informed, responsible participants in shaping the world we all share.

HOW IT WORKS

In exploring what's most important when it comes to teaching students about AI, the Organisation for Economic Co-operation and Development takes the stance that preparing students for the future means building their capacity to navigate complexity, reflect on change, and take part in shaping ethical and inclusive societies, not just perform well on academic tasks (Schleicher, 2018). Just as we teach students to analyze sources, engage in meaningful dialogue, and apply academic skills to face-to-face situations, we must also teach them to understand, question, and engage with the technologies shaping their lives. Teaching about AI in society is not extra; it's essential.

> ### Common Classroom Applications
>
> #### Elementary Examples
>
> - **Have students brainstorm ways AI might be used in school (autocorrect, book recommendations, daily tasks like lunch count or attendance).** From there have students sort the ideas into categories like *very helpful*, *somewhat helpful*, or *not helpful at all*. Use this to talk about the positive and negative aspects of AI in society.
>
> *(Continued)*

(Continued)

- **Explore an AI-powered tool already used in the classroom.** Guide students to investigate how it "knows" what to do next. Ask, "How does it decide what to recommend? What information does it use?" This builds awareness of how AI personalizes learning experiences.
- **Analyze AI-generated images.** Show students examples that appear real but include small clues that they were made by AI. Invite them to look closely and explain how they know and why that matters in a world where images can be manipulated.

Secondary Examples

- **Read and respond to a current article about AI integration in society.** The daily news is filled with articles about self-driving cars, facial recognition, or medical technology, to name but a few possible topics. Have students identify both benefits and concerns, then write an opinion piece or debate whether the AI use described is helpful, harmful, or a mix of both.
- **Foster AI career exploration.** Students interested in learning more about careers can investigate how AI has impacted their selected industry. Students may initially (and inaccurately) believe that AI is only impacting technology careers. The World Economic Forum *Future of Jobs Report* estimates that 86 percent of jobs will be reshaped by 2030 (WEF, 2025) and calls for a "reskilling revolution." Among the most heavily impacted? Farmworkers, construction workers, and nurses.

Strategy in Action

Incorporate a lesson on how artificial intelligence is used in civic systems, for example, in voting, law enforcement, or public service programs. While teaching about civics, address the ways this technology can affect fairness and access across a system. The class reads a variety of texts explaining how these technologies are used and may even talk with the school nurse, a voting commissioner, a parent in a technology field, or other local stakeholders who can help explain how these systems work in their own community. Students then engage in a guided discussion to analyze how AI is being used, who it helps, who might be at risk, and whether it aligns with the values and goals of that civic system. By connecting this learning to a topic already being taught, the teacher helps students explore real examples of where AI is showing up, shaping society, and raising questions about how we respond.

Teacher Moves

- Select content you are exploring with students in a unit or lesson and find a current example of AI being used in an area connected to that content. Provide specific examples of how and where AI is integrated into this part of society.

- Provide guiding questions for a structured discussion, such as, "Who is impacted by this? What values or goals does it support or challenge?"

Student Moves

- When relevant, join students in investigating how AI is impacting the topic of study, whether it is zoo management in biology, examining survey data in math, or reading a picture book with illustrations and photographs.

- Students can interview a family member or community worker about their experiences or concerns with AI.

- Have learners compare how AI is used in different countries and discuss equity or access issues.

Extension or Adaptation Idea

- **Advanced learners:** Generate a list of related topics or questions connected to the issue being studied (for example, surveillance, public trust, or bias), and choose one to investigate further through research or discussion.

- **Multilingual learners:** Ask students to label images showing AI in daily life (e.g., smart home, chatbots, GPS) and explain their function orally.

- **Emerging readers:** Use a short video about robots or AI helpers and draw what they learned, then annotate or highlight key ideas together.

- **Cross-content:** Students create visual representations of how AI might change their community in the next twenty years, combining creative expression with future-focused thinking, and explain their choices in a short artist's statement.

Skill Progression by Grade Band

Grade Band	Skills	Supports
K–2: Noticing Technology in the World	• Identify tools and machines in their everyday life (including smart tools) • Talk about how people use technology to help them • Recognize that AI is created by people	• **Picture walks or classroom hunts for "smart" tools** • Read-alouds featuring technology helpers (real or fictional) • Sorting activity: "Made by people" vs. "Used by people"

(Continued)

(Continued)

Grade Band	Skills	Supports
3–5: Exploring the Role of AI in Daily Life	• Give examples of how AI is used in homes, schools, or communities • Ask questions about how and why AI is used • Begin to wonder who creates AI and why	• **"Where do we see AI?" chart for guided exploration** • Sentence starters for curiosity: "What if AI . . . ?" or "Who decides . . . ?" • Videos or visuals of everyday AI use (voice assistants, recommendations, etc.)
6–8: Considering Impact and Influence	• Analyze how AI affects decisions in school, home, or society • Discuss who benefits from AI and who might be left out • Identify ways AI shapes habits, choices, or opportunities	• **Short scenarios of AI in action with guided reflection and analysis** • Discussion protocols for fairness, bias, and access • Graphic organizers for tracking positives and concerns
9–12: Investigating Ethics, Equity, and Systems	• Evaluate the societal impact of AI in areas like education, health care, justice, and media • Explore issues of data use, privacy, and algorithmic bias	• **Protocol and topics for debate around AI and society** • Tools for analyzing who benefits or is harmed by AI decisions • Access to news articles, expert interviews, and data-driven reports for research

Examples of the boldface supports above can be found on the book's companion website here: https://companion.corwin.com/courses/TeachingStudentsAI

Section 2

Teaching *for* AI

Developing Human Intelligence Skills in Students

OVERVIEW

When the world changes, so do the skills required to survive and thrive in it. From the agricultural era to the printing press, from the Industrial Revolution to the Digital Age, each major societal shift has required new ways of thinking and working. The current change that we are confronting and learning to embrace is the AI revolution. In this new reality, we cannot simply prepare students for a specific career or a fixed future. We must prepare them to adapt, retool, and reinvent themselves continually. In short, we must teach *for* AI by developing learners who are future-proof, not just future-ready.

As we described in the book's opening, teaching in the age of AI is like watching something massive surface just beyond the boat. It's powerful, hard to predict, and mostly hidden beneath the waterline. What's visible are tools like chatbots and image generators. What's less obvious are the skills students need to use these tools with integrity, curiosity, and critical judgment. That's where this section begins.

According to the World Economic Forum's *Future of Jobs Report* (2024), the skills needed for success in the near future are quickly changing. They categorize these skills into four types:

- **Core Skills for 2030:** Foundational capabilities like critical thinking, problem-solving, and communication.
- **Emerging Skills:** Skills gaining importance due to technological change, such as AI literacy and systems thinking.
- **Steady Skills:** Skills with lasting value like collaboration, empathy, and leadership.
- **Out-of-Focus Skills:** Skills decreasing in relevance, often tied to routine tasks or outdated systems.

For educators, these categories require that we examine how our instruction aligns with the world students will enter. Two standout examples from the "emerging" list are curiosity and cognitive flexibility, which are skills teachers have nurtured in classrooms, but which now have increased importance as AI tools reshape how we learn and work.

One area where we respectfully disagree with the WEF report is the suggestion that reading, writing, and math are becoming less essential. These core competencies are more critical than ever. They are gateway skills that allow students to engage meaningfully with AI. Consider this: A student with limited reading comprehension may accept a chatbot's response without question. A student with strong literacy skills can evaluate, revise, and improve what AI suggests. Likewise, students who understand mathematical reasoning are better equipped to analyze AI-generated graphs, interpret data, and challenge flawed conclusions. Far from being obsolete, literacy and numeracy are critical aspects of the human-AI collaboration.

AI can write, summarize, and compute. It was created to mimic human brains and our neural network, which is why they have many of the same quirks that we have. Today, even the most advanced models/neural nets are still far simpler than the human brain. But these systems have less to do than our brains and far more digital data to train on. They don't have to regulate or move a complex body. They also don't adapt in real time the way a brain does. The human brain needs to learn how to use AI systems which means guiding students to

- Read to distinguish fact from fiction, bias from objectivity, and human voice from machine output.

- Write with intention to record their thoughts and to generate, refine, and communicate ideas clearly.

- Think mathematically by seeing patterns, modeling scenarios, and verifying AI's calculations with logical rigor.

Doing so requires a number of skills that do have increased importance in the AI world in which our students live. We have profiled 13 of those skills in this section, each of which will contribute to students' ability to use, learn from, and learn with AI systems.

SECTION 2 • TEACHING *FOR* AI

Figure 1 • The Core Skills for 2030

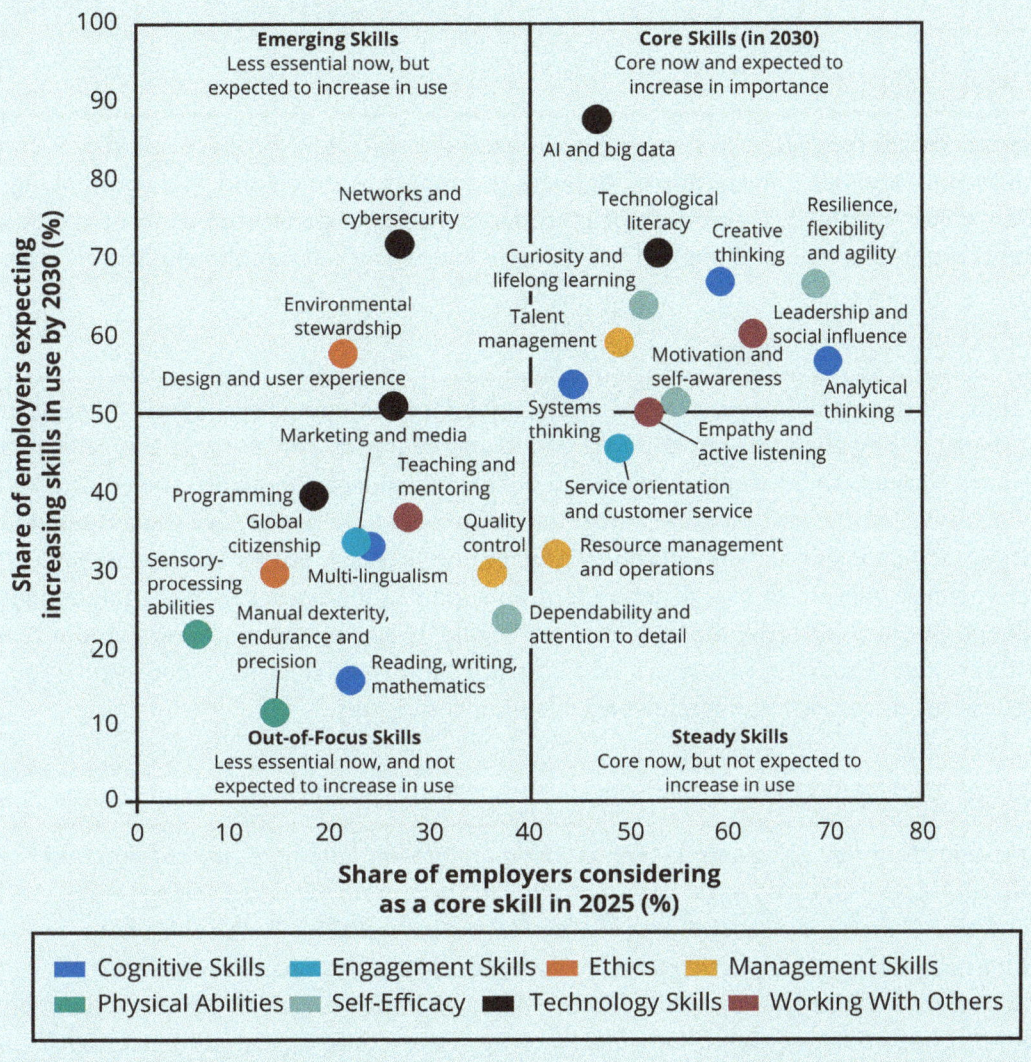

Source: World Economic Forum. (2024). *The future of jobs report 2025*. https://www.weforum.org/publications/the-future-of-jobs-report-2025/

Information Literacy

WHAT IS IT?

Information literacy (IL) skills are the abilities students use to locate, evaluate, understand, and use information effectively to support learning and decision-making. When working with AI, these skills help students interpret generated content critically, extract what is useful, and apply it responsibly inside and outside the classroom walls.

WHY IT MATTERS

IL skills are essential because they empower students to navigate the vast amount of information they encounter in both academic and everyday contexts. These skills help learners distinguish between reliable and unreliable sources, evaluate the relevance and accuracy of content, and use information purposefully to support their thinking, writing, and problem-solving. Without information literacy, students may become overwhelmed, misled, or overly dependent on superficial answers rather than engaging in deeper inquiry. As students develop these skills, they become more independent, confident, and thoughtful learners who can make informed decisions, contribute to discussions, and adapt to complex and evolving challenges.

HOW IT WORKS

IL includes four key components: *recognizing an information need, identifying and evaluating sources, using information effectively*, and *creating and sharing new knowledge* (American Association of School Librarians, 2025). These skills help students become active participants in learning, rather than passive users of AI-generated content. When students use AI to explore ideas or complete assignments, they first need to clarify what information they are seeking. This step focuses their inquiry and helps them avoid vague or unfocused prompts that often lead to confusion.

The second component, information identification and evaluation, is especially important because AI tools do not always produce accurate or current information. Students must learn to assess whether AI responses are useful and trustworthy through digital source evaluation (Merga & Mat Roni, 2025).

Once students locate appropriate information, they must decide how to use it. This includes summarizing, combining ideas, and applying knowledge to a task in a way that reflects their own thinking (National Research Council, 2000).

Finally, learners often use AI to support content creation. They might write reports, design presentations, or develop arguments with help from AI. Information literacy ensures that students make ethical choices about what they share and how they present it. In this way, IL supports the responsible use of AI and strengthens students' independence as learners. Subsequent features in this section will explore specific elements of information literacy in more detail.

Common Classroom Applications

Elementary Examples

- **Model curiosity, using question starters.** Encourage students to voice or write their questions to set the foundation for identifying an information need. Anchor charts and group discussions can guide students in forming clear, purposeful questions.

- **Build the habit of identifying sources and verifying information.** Introduce simple questions such as, "Who made this?" and "Is it meant to teach or sell?" Compare books, videos, and AI-generated responses so students can practice judging usefulness and clarity.

- **Show students how to organize and apply what they learn.** Use graphic organizers, model how to take notes in their own words, and ask students to combine information from multiple sources.

- **Create opportunities to share what they've learned responsibly.** Offer real audiences and encourage students to give credit to their sources, including digital tools.

Secondary Examples

- **Strengthen the framing of information needs.** Help students move from vague curiosity to clear, researchable questions. Encourage students to define their information need with academic, personal, and creative purposes. In science, for example, students can define what kind of data or background information they need before starting a lab.

- **Deepen evaluation of sources and AI outputs.** Facilitate lessons where students evaluate conflicting sources or compare AI-generated content with vetted academic materials. In digital contexts, students can use AI as a first draft tool but must explain why they accept or reject specific responses.

- **Promote strategic information use.** Require students to organize information into arguments that demonstrate synthesis and decision-making. Instead of copying and pasting, students should paraphrase, annotate, and combine multiple sources, including AI-generated summaries, into cohesive interpretations.

- **Emphasize ethical creation and distribution.** As students use AI to create content, emphasize academic integrity, originality, and audience awareness. Lessons can include how to properly cite AI as a source, when its use is appropriate, and how to identify overreliance on automated tools.

Strategy in Action

To teach students how to organize and summarize AI-generated content, begin by selecting a sample AI response to a question related to the topic you are teaching, and project it for the class to examine. Model a think-aloud process, highlighting sentences that directly answer the question, identifying off-topic or redundant parts, and annotating unclear phrasing. Use a color-coded system (e.g., yellow for key ideas, blue for supporting details, red for irrelevant information), and demonstrate how to deconstruct the response and extract only the meaningful information.

Next, students work in pairs to apply the same process to a different AI-generated paragraph, using graphic organizers such as a main idea detail web to structure the content. Once students identify key information, introduce a summary frame (e.g., "This response explains that ___ because ___, and gives the example of ___."), encouraging them to paraphrase rather than copy.

Throughout the lesson, lead discussions on *why* certain information is more important, helping students learn to prioritize based on their purpose. Prompt students to notice when the AI's answer is vague or inflated with filler phrases, reinforcing that part of summarizing is deciding what *not* to keep. As a final step, students reflect on how their summary changed or improved the original content, reinforcing their role as editors and decision-makers rather than passive users.

Teacher Moves

- Assign reflective prompts such as, "How did using AI shape your thinking?" or "What choices did you make to make this your own?"
- Ask, "What is missing here?" or "What perspective does this information leave out?"
- Require students to cite sources with their work.

Student Moves

- Have students highlight useful versus irrelevant information in a text or AI response.
- Provide choice in how students demonstrate their learning (poster, slide deck, essay).
- Teach lessons that require students to ask follow-up questions to the chatbot to clarify unclear or suspicious claims.

Extensions and Adaptations

- **Advanced learners:** Have students critique the reliability and limitations of AI as a source. Give them the choice of format and provide them an audience to present to.

INFORMATION LITERACY

- **Multilingual learners:** Model how to cite AI as a helper, making it apparent when it is used to generate content.
- **Emerging readers:** Limit outputs to short, focused responses, then guide students in summarizing the meaning.
- **Cross-content:** Instruct students to evaluate how AI-generated information shifts depending on disciplinary context; for example, how do the chatbot answers about the concept of freedom in history compare to those in science and in narrative literature.

Skill Progression by Grade Band

Grade Band	Skills	Supports
K–2: Learning to Wonder	<ul><li>Recognize when you want to learn something</li><li>Sort information learned into different categories</li><li>Share simple facts learned</li></ul>	<ul><li>**Visual organizer using icons and symbols**</li><li>Read-aloud options with guided questioning</li><li>Picture-based graphic organizers</li><li>Shared writing prompts</li></ul>
3–5: Exploring and Organizing Ideas	<ul><li>Generate focused questions for a topic before, during, and after reading</li><li>Identify basic facts and main ideas</li><li>Organize notes by topic</li><li>Summarize information for different audience</li></ul>	<ul><li>Sentence stems for asking and summarizing</li><li>**Note-taking templates**</li><li>Lessons on summarizing and paraphrasing AI content</li></ul>
6–8: Managing Information for a Purpose	<ul><li>Refine research questions for clarity</li><li>Identify relevant details from multiple sources</li><li>Synthesize ideas into structured outlines</li><li>Decide what details best support a position or explain a process</li></ul>	<ul><li>Graphic organizers for source comparison and synthesis</li><li>Lessons on summarizing and paraphrasing AI content</li><li>**Checklists for reading information and organizing thinking**</li></ul>
9–12: Creating With Intent	<ul><li>Define complex information needs</li><li>Manage and organize multiple forms of content</li><li>Summarize and integrate information into original work</li><li>Create and share content with a specific purpose or audience in mind</li></ul>	<ul><li>Planning tools for multi-source projects</li><li>Templates for integrating citations (including AI)</li><li>**Student thinking and reflection prompts on information use**</li></ul>

 Examples of the boldface supports above can be found on the book's companion website here: https://companion.corwin.com/courses/TeachingStudentsAI

Data Literacy

WHAT IS IT?

Data literacy is the ability to read, write, analyze, and communicate with data. It's about understanding what data means, how to interpret it, and how to effectively present findings. In essence, it's the capacity to work with data like you would with written words, deriving meaning and acting on it.

WHY IT MATTERS

In the context of AI, data are what systems are trained on and what directly shapes the output they generate. In a world where content is constantly being created and shared, helping students evaluate and make sense of it is essential. Not all data are accurate, complete, or useful. Data literacy is a critical skill for students to develop as they begin working with AI tools in the classroom. As AI becomes more integrated into learning, students need to understand how to think critically about the data that powers these tools.

Data literacy isn't a collection of skills, it's a mindset. It's a way of thinking critically and analytically about the information we take in and what we choose to create or make of that information. In the context of generative AI, this means teaching students not just to accept what AI produces, but to slow down and ask, Where did this data come from? How was it shaped? What do I do with it?

HOW IT WORKS

Data literacy is an essential skill for students, especially as they begin to work with AI tools in the classroom. Research shows that students who understand how to question, analyze, and reflect on data are better equipped for critical thinking and problem-solving (Gummer & Mandinach, 2015). The first element of data literacy is *data exploration*, where students learn to consider the purpose behind the data they are using or generating. This helps develop digital and ethical awareness, a key part of 21st-century competencies. *Data management* involves collecting and organizing data responsibly, which is a necessary skill in environments where students interact with AI systems that rely on user-generated inputs. With *data use*, students learn to interpret data patterns and apply findings to authentic problems, supporting deeper learning and metacognitive development (Means et al., 2010). The final element, *reflection and improvement*, encourages students to evaluate their own processes and make informed decisions about how to improve. This four-part cycle, developed by the National Center for Systematic Improvement in 2021, allows students to become not just consumers of technology, but thoughtful, empowered learners prepared for future academic and professional challenges.

Common Classroom Applications

Elementary Examples

- **Ask AI to create a chart from class data.** Students collect simple data, such as favorite fruits or playground activities, and input it into an AI tool that creates a chart. They discuss how the data was organized and whether the visual accurately represents the class preferences.

- **Use AI to sort and classify data.** Students use an AI image recognition tool to sort pictures of animals by habitat. This helps them practice data exploration by asking why certain data (like animal type or environment) matters, and how organizing it supports learning.

Secondary Examples

- **Use AI to analyze survey results.** Students design and distribute a short schoolwide survey to classmates, then input the results into an AI tool that visualizes trends or patterns. They interpret the visualizations to draw conclusions using large datasets, developing skills in data use and purposeful analysis.

- **Compare AI predictions to real data.** Students use an AI simulation to predict plant growth under different conditions (light, water, soil). They then grow real plants under similar conditions and compare the AI's predictions to their observed results, analyzing discrepancies in data and reflecting on model accuracy.

Strategy in Action

To help students build data literacy while learning about generative AI, introduce a routine called "What's Behind the Answer?" Use a simplified decision-making tool adapted from UNESCO's *Guidance for Generative AI in Education* (Miao & Holmes, 2023), helping students ask, "Does it matter if this is true?" and "Do I have what I need to check it?" to investigate the accuracy of AI-generated data analysis. After students use an AI tool to analyze a dataset, such as calculating averages, creating graphs, or identifying trends, they are prompted to reflect on the output using the two questions. For example, in a math or science class, students might input survey results or experiment data into an AI tool to generate a line graph showing a trend over time.

Students then ask, "Does it matter if this trend is accurate?" Recognizing that incorrect trends can lead to false conclusions, such as misidentifying whether a variable affects an outcome, is crucial. They follow up by again posing the question, "Do I have what I need to check it?" by recalculating key statistics (like mean or range), manually graphing a portion of the data, or comparing the AI's chart to their

(Continued)

(Continued)

own visual analysis. This strategy helps students develop the habit of not accepting AI outputs at face value, and positions reflection as an essential part of responsible data use and improvement.

Teacher Moves

- Model always taking the time to pause and think aloud, "What's behind this answer?" when interacting with any data, whether it is AI-generated or not.
- Use real or pre-generated examples to highlight bias, gaps, or assumptions in output.
- Teach students how to use tools, such as the decision-making frame, as a cueing system when building their data literacy.

Student Moves

- Have learners explain how the data supports or contradicts a claim.
- Students can compare AI-generated graphs with hand-drawn versions to check accuracy.
- Add a question to assignments to prompt reflection on whether the data collected actually answers their original question.

Extension or Adaptation Idea

- **Advanced learners:** Challenge students to compare data outputs from multiple AI tools, evaluate discrepancies, and write a justification of which tool provided the most reliable or valid analysis.
- **Multilingual learners:** Have students translate and compare data representations (e.g., charts, graphs, tables) from different languages or cultural contexts, then evaluate how language or presentation choices influence interpretation.
- **Emerging readers:** Use pictographs, number lines, and color-coded charts generated with AI, then ask students to interpret the visuals with teacher or peer support.
- **Cross-content:** In a social studies and math crossover, students analyze population or economic data from different countries using AI tools, then write or present evidence-based claims about global trends.

Skill Progression by Grade Band

Grade Band	Skills	Supports
K–2: Everyday Noticers	• Notice how information is collected and used in daily life (classroom, games, apps) • Recognize that different kinds of information (numbers, words, images) tell us something • Begin asking simple questions like, "Where did this come from?"	• Collection of classroom data (weather charts, lunch count) to talk about how we collect and use info • "What do you notice?" picture sort using images, graphs, and symbols • **Data detective chart to help guide students in data look-fors**
3–5: Data Meaning-Makers	• Identify data in the world around them (polls, records, search results) • Begin to ask what the data shows and what might be missing • Reflect on how AI tools might use data to make guesses	• **Graphic organizer: "What I see/What it might mean"** • Class analysis of simple charts or AI-generated content • Sentence frames for questioning data: "Could this be wrong?" "What else do I need to know?"
6–8: Data Questioners	• Explain how data shapes AI responses • Ask questions about source, bias, and what's left out in datasets • Compare different outputs and consider how input or training data influenced them	• Side-by-side comparison: Same prompt, different outputs • Annotation tasks: "What's fact, what's filler, what's missing?" • **Red flags in data chart and examples**
9–12: Critical Data Thinkers	• Analyze data sources behind AI-generated content • Communicate what the data show and what might be missing or misrepresented	• Case study analysis using authentic outputs and datasets • Claim-evidence reasoning tasks tied to AI-generated data responses • **Source analysis and data use reflection tool**

 Examples of the boldface supports above can be found on the book's companion website here: https://companion.corwin.com/courses/TeachingStudentsAI

Questioning

WHAT IS IT?

Student-generated questions allow students to develop and practice a variety of cognitive processes such as to synthesize, clarify, analyze, evaluate, and reflect.

WHY IT MATTERS

Encouraging students to ask questions is not new but has been increasingly important as students interact with artificial intelligence systems. When students ask questions, they engage more deeply with the content and are often more motivated to learn. Inviting students to generate questions has been shown to improve test scores (Teplitski et al., 2018), reading comprehension (Fordham, 2006), and motivation (Minigan et al., 2017). When students know how to ask questions, especially questions that remain on topic, are focused, and specific to their needs, their AI systems are more likely to respond with useful results. Generally speaking, there are two types of questions that students (and teachers) can ask: open and closed.

> *Open questions* have many acceptable answers and often begin with words like *how, why, in what ways,* or *what do you think about.* They encourage explanation, interpretation, analysis, or reflection.

> *Closed questions* have a limited number of acceptable responses and are used to confirm understanding, or gather quick, specific answers. Open questions are not better than closed questions as they serve different purposes. Both can focus on higher or lower levels of thinking.

Feature	Open-Ended Questions	Closed-Ended Questions
Response Type	Detailed, explanatory	Brief, specific
Thinking Required	Higher-order thinking (analyze, reflect, etc.)	Lower-order thinking (recall, recognize)
Examples	"Why did that solution work?"	"Did that solution work?"
Purpose	Encourage discussion, exploration	Check for understanding or facts
Flexibility	Multiple possible answers	One correct or expected answer

HOW IT WORKS

Children know how to ask questions. They ask over 40,000 questions between the ages of two and five, averaging 25 questions per waking hour (Harris, 2015). Engel (2015) notes, "What begins as a robust characteristic, possessed by all normally developing babies, becomes more fragile . . . and is hard to find at all by the time children are in elementary school" (p. 2). Thus, the goal is to maintain the natural question-asking tendencies that they already have. The Question Formation Technique (Rothstein & Santana, 2011) has been used with learners across ages and includes the following steps:

1. **Start With a Question Focus.** The teacher shows something interesting—a picture, video, or object—to spark curiosity.

2. **Ask as Many Questions as You Can.** Students brainstorm lots of questions about the prompt. If they generate statements, these are revised into questions.

3. **Sort the Questions.** Students figure out which questions are open-ended (need explanation) and which are closed-ended (yes/no or short answers).

4. **Identify the Most Important Questions.** Students choose the best or most interesting questions to focus on and discuss why they matter.

5. **Reflect on the Process.** Students talk about what they learned from asking and choosing questions.

6. **Use the Questions to Learn More.** Students explore answers by reading, researching, or doing an activity.

> ## Common Classroom Applications
>
> ### Elementary Examples
>
> - **Use text to backward-engineer questions.** Have students submit a piece of text they have written or found and then ask the chatbot to generate questions. They can ask for open and closed questions or questions that are literal and inferential, then answer the generated questions.
>
> - **Use pictures to foster questions.** Give students engaging pictures related to the topic you are teaching and ask them to generate as many questions as they can. Then have them sort the questions by type: "Questions with one right answer" versus "Questions that make us think more."
>
> ### Secondary Examples
>
> - **Ask students to start a topical conversation with their chatbot.** Instruct them that they must ask three follow-up questions and analyze the responses. They should submit the transcript for review to determine the types of questions they ask so that future question generation lessons can be developed.
>
> - **Create a wonder wall.** Encourage students to post questions on the wall so that question generation is normalized within the environment. Spend time each week selecting questions to discuss. Provide students time to engage their AI systems with the questions they and others post on the wonder wall.

Strategy in Action

The question-answer relationship (QAR) framework has been used to teach students that there is a connection between the type of question they ask and the location of the answer (Raphael et al., 2006). The four-part framework can be used to teach students the types of questions they can use to prompt their AI systems to obtain the information they want.

QAR Question Type	Description	AI Adaptation	Sample Prompt
Right There	The answer is found directly in the text.	Ask specific, fact-based questions.	What is the largest planet in our solar system?
Think and Search	The answer is in several parts of the text.	Ask questions that require comparing or combining information.	How are rivers and oceans similar and different?
Author and You	Use both what the text says and your own thinking.	Ask reflective questions that mix AI input with your ideas.	Why do some animals migrate, and how does that affect ecosystems?
On My Own	The answer comes from your own experience.	Ask for suggestions or ideas based on your interests.	What are some ways people adapt to living in deserts?

Teacher Moves

- Think aloud as you pose questions while reading or problem-solving: "I wonder why . . . ?" or "What would happen if . . . ?
- Highlight different question types during a range of lessons and invite students to generate questions as part of their class activities.
- Provide verbs that can be used in question stems such as *compare*, *explain*, *evaluate*, *predict*, or *design*.

Student Moves

- Keep track of questions as they arise, in a notebook or online tool.
- Learn to analyze the questions (open and closed) and the type of responses expected from AI.
- Invite students to critique peer questions for clarity, depth, and relevance and provide growth-producing feedback to peers to improve their questioning skills.

> ### Extensions and Adaptations
>
> - **Advanced learners:** Require that they rewrite questions with increased levels of academic vocabulary. For example, rather than "What is photosynthesis?" they might write, "Describe the role and process of photosynthesis."
>
> - **Multilingual learners:** Provide question stems for students to use such as, "Why do you think . . . ?" "What would happen if . . . ?" "How might we . . . ?" "What is the difference between . . . and . . . ?" Use visuals or posters of question stems for reference.
>
> - **Emerging readers:** Use puppets or role-play to model asking questions. Invite students to ask the puppet questions.
>
> - **Cross-content:** Ask students to generate questions that require knowledge of different subjects (e.g., "How does geography affect the rise of civilizations?").

Skill Progression by Grade Band

Grade Band	Skills	Supports
K–2: Encouraging Curiosity and Questioning Through Play	• Ask different kinds of questions based on tasks (e.g., reading stories, doing experiments, or having discussions) • Differentiate between asking and telling • Recognize that questions can start with who, what, when, where, why, or how • Respond to questions in different ways that match the purpose of learning	• **Role-play scenarios to model the difference between asking and telling** • Sentence stems and question starters for questioning and responding • Collection of student questions during read-alouds or lessons for later discussion • Routines for sharing "wonderings" and "noticings"
3–5: Building Awareness of Open vs. Closed Questions	• Distinguish between open and closed questions • Use visual prompts or texts to generate multiple types of questions • Sort questions by type and choose the most useful ones for learning • Use AI to test and revise their questions based on the quality of responses	• **Charts to compare open vs. closed questions** • Sentence starters grouped by purpose (e.g., clarify, evaluate, compare) • Lessons on the Questions Formation Technique (QFT) • AI-generated questions for sorts and guided discussions

(Continued)

(Continued)

Grade Band	Skills	Supports
6–8: Expanding Question Purpose and Structure	• Generate follow-up questions during AI conversations • Question intentionally to explore a topic (e.g., clarify vs. challenge) • Use frameworks like QAR or QFT to classify and improve questions • Analyze peer questions for clarity, purpose, and depth	• **QAR charts and real examples of student-AI interactions** • Peer-feedback rubrics for evaluating question clarity and depth • Model questioning during reading, writing, or discussions • Prompt students to reflect on what their questions helped them discover
9–12: Designing Strategic, Cross-Disciplinary Questions	• Craft purposeful, discipline-specific questions to prompt AI systems • Generate multi-step, layered questions for deeper inquiry • Critique AI responses to improve their own questioning techniques • Use academic vocabulary in question stems to enhance precision	• Academic verb charts to support high-level questioning • Tools to track and improve question quality over time • **Question-focused prompt analysis and evaluation tool** • Cross-curricular tasks that require generating interdisciplinary questions

 Examples of the boldface supports above can be found on the book's companion website here: https://companion.corwin.com/courses/TeachingStudentsAI

Prompt Engineering

WHAT IS IT?

Prompt engineering is the art and practice of developing clear, purposeful initial prompts that guide AI output. Prompts help students engage with AI in ways that support learning, creativity, and deeper thinking. Prompts are more than asking a question, as was common in using search engines. Instead, prompts focus on the information needed from the AI system. Language input is used to generate meaningful output. That means the quality of the AI system's response is shaped by the quality of the prompt. Vague, underdeveloped prompts often lead to generic, confusing, or unhelpful answers.

WHY IT MATTERS

In a world where students increasingly engage with AI tools to brainstorm, explain, create, and solve problems, teaching them to write strong prompts is not optional. It's an essential skill that can be taught and practiced. Prompt engineering is more than a technology skill. It's also a literacy skill because students must use their language, logic, and learning to successfully craft prompts. Analyzing student prompts is a great source of assessment information. The kinds of prompts students write reveal what they understand, what they're curious about, and where their thinking might still be unclear. This analysis can guide future instruction in prompt writing as well as in content learning.

HOW IT WORKS

There are several prompt structures that can be taught. For example, Context, Ask, Rules, and Examples (Moran, 2024) teaches students to consider the situation (context), add a request (ask), outline any constraints or rules the chatbot should follow (rules), and conclude with the desired outcome (examples).

- **Context:** Describe the situation, background, or relevant information. This helps the AI understand the task and generate more relevant responses.
- **Ask:** Clearly state the specific action you want the AI to perform. Be precise and avoid ambiguity.
- **Rules:** Define any constraints or limitations on the AI's response, such as length, format, tone, or style.
- **Examples:** Provide examples of the desired output format or content. This helps the AI learn and produce responses that match your expectations.

Common Classroom Applications

Elementary Examples

- **Review or summarize texts.** Students can write their own summaries of a passage and then prompt the AI (e.g., "Summarize this paragraph in one sentence") to compare, contrast, and revise.
- **Practice perspective taking.** Use AI to role-play characters, historical figures, or points of view. For example, "Write a conversation between two minor characters from the story."

Secondary Examples

- **Reword content for clarity.** Students can prompt AI to reword something to help them better understand a complex concept. For example, "Explain photosynthesis to a 5th grader using a fun metaphor."
- **Solving math or science problems with explanations.** Use AI to model thinking, explain steps, or offer multiple solution paths. For example, "Explain how to solve $3(x + 2) = 15$ step-by-step."

Strategy in Action

In writing, students are often confronted with a blank page, which can be frustrating and prevent them from getting started with their writing. AI can serve as a brainstorming partner to help the student generate ideas to write about. Consider modeling both weak and stronger prompts, such as

- Weak prompt: *Give me a story idea.*
- Stronger prompt: *Give me three story ideas for a realistic fiction story about a kid who just moved to a new city and wants to make friends.*

Together, the class can analyze the differences, including the specificity, the genre, and the character situation. Students can then work individually or with a partner to generate ideas based on the prompt they have supplied to their AI system.

Teacher Moves

- Model prompt editing by starting with a vague prompt and then improving it together.
- Create a prompt gallery on a classroom wall.
- Create a class "prompt ladder" from simpler to more specific and strategic characteristics.
- Pair students to peer review prompts before using them.

Student Moves

- Brainstorm vocabulary or details they might include in their prompt.
- Use a prompt builder template.
- Use verbs like *explain*, *compare*, *summarize*, or *in the voice of* . . .
- Set a tone or identify an audience: "Write for a 3rd grader."
- Rate and revise their own prompts based on output quality.
- Reflect in journals: "How did the AI help me think differently?"

Extension or Adaptation

- **Advanced learners:** Create "multi-turn" prompts with follow-ups. Rather than stop after one prompt-response cycle, challenge students to extend the conversation by asking follow-up questions, rephrasing, or requesting the AI to consider new angles.
- **Multilingual learners:** Use voice-to-text tools for prompting. Allow students to speak their prompts using built-in voice-to-text tools or AI-integrated apps. For example, the student says, *"Explica el ciclo del agua en inglés con palabras fáciles."*
- **Emerging readers:** Use sentence starters, picture cues, or drag-and-drop tiles to help younger or developing readers build their prompts.
- **Cross-content:** Compare how prompting works in English Language Arts versus science. Teach students to adapt their prompt style depending on content and purpose. In ELA, prompts might ask for tone, voice, or character analysis. In science, prompts might ask for clarity, process, or explanation.

Skill Progression by Grade Band

Grade Band	Skills	Supports
K–2: Foundations of Asking for Help and Clarifying Ideas	<ul><li>Use sentence stems to request help (e.g., "Tell me about . . . ")</li><li>Choose from pictures or icons to build a question</li><li>Verbally dictate a question with teacher or voice support</li><li>Recognize when a response is helpful or confusing</li><li>Ask for more information by sharing what you already know</li></ul>	<ul><li>Sentence starters and cue cards that match the different components of successful AI prompts</li><li>Class "Wonder Wall" of prompts</li><li>Voice-to-text tools for student practice</li><li>**Collection of images with varying levels of detail to guide discussions of prompting techniques**</li></ul>

(Continued)

(Continued)

Grade Band	Skills	Supports
3–5: Moving From Asking Questions to Designing Prompts	• Use carefully selected verbs to guide AI responses • Add context to prompts based on purpose • Include format requests (e.g., list, paragraph, questions and answers) • Evaluate AI output and revise prompts based on clarity or relevance • Begin using CARE (Context, Ask, Rules, Examples) with scaffolding	• Class anchor charts with "Strong vs. Weak Prompts" • Peer review or partner revision of prompts • Role-playing scenarios on how AI "thinks" for student practice • **Collection of AI outputs that can be used for sorting, discussion, and practice**
6–8: Prompting With Purpose, Feedback, and Iteration	• Write multi-part prompts using all CARE elements • Use AI to brainstorm, reword, compare, or explain with constraints • Create "what if" or "explain like . . ." prompts to deepen understanding • Generate and test multiple versions of the same prompt • Begin cross-content prompting (e.g., science vs. ELA tasks)	• Prompt revision checklists • Discussion prompts for AI accuracy and output evaluation • Role-play scenarios to practice follow-up questioning and prompting • **CARE writing framework guide and prompt building templates**
9–12: Advancing Strategic Questioning	• Independently craft high-quality prompts using CARE or other structures • Apply different prompt styles based on audience, tone, and domain • Use follow-up prompting and multi-turn conversations to refine responses • Design prompts for creative tasks (e.g., speeches, scripts) • Analyze AI responses for bias, limitations, and logic • Teach or coach others on effective prompting (peer mentorship)	• **Comparison tasks: "Which prompt works better, and why?"** • Interdisciplinary project prompts • Collection of AI-generated debates for practice of follow-up prompting • Tools for prompt planning, testing, and evaluation

 Examples of the boldface supports above can be found on the book's companion website here: https://companion.corwin.com/courses/TeachingStudentsAI

Dialogue

WHAT IS IT?

Dialogue in AI involves asking clear, purposeful questions and responding thoughtfully to guide the chatbot toward deeper understanding and more relevant outcomes. Students use argumentation skills which include agreeing and disagreeing in respectful ways, asking for clarity or additional information, and requesting source information.

WHY IT MATTERS

As social animals, humans learn a lot through their interactions with other humans. We consolidate our understanding during these interactions, and we use dialogue to keep the interactions moving forward. AI systems and chatbots are built on the same idea. Users interact with them, through dialogue, rather than simply searching for information as was common with search engines. As Ostroff (2020) notes, "Learning in dialogue runs deep in the human race; the oral traditions of our ancestors took place not in passive transactions, but in asking questions, deliberating, sharing experiences, and negotiating truths" (p. 15). These skills are crucial when it comes to interacting with artificial intelligence systems.

We have already addressed student-generated questions. But dialogue is more than that. It's the give-and-take, back-and-forth interaction in which better information and understanding is produced. As Ostroff noted, it's also about negotiating truths. The initial responses of AI systems are just that, a good starting place. However, without sustained dialogue, students may simply accept that their chatbot has produced accurate and complete information. As Zhai et al. (2024) note, "individuals increasingly favor fast and optimal solutions over slow ones constrained by practicality" (p. 28). Teachers can build students' dialogue skills to ensure that they take the time to carefully consider the output, applying their argumentation skills, while also learning content.

HOW IT WORKS

Dialogue leads to discussion. It's a skill that develops over our lifespan. When teachers foster this skill, students can apply it in interactions with other people and with their AI systems. And the AI systems can help students develop better skills for interacting with humans. In this way, artificial intelligence is fostering human intelligence and human intelligence is used to improve the responses from artificial intelligence. There are several factors that contribute to a quality discussion (e.g., Fisher et al., 2008) that can be taught and practiced, and then applied to AI dialogue.

Guideline	What It Looks Like	Sample Language
Listen to Understand	Focus on the speaker. Don't interrupt. Use body language that shows listening.	"So you're saying that . . ." "I heard you mention . . ."
Speak Clearly and Respectfully	Use a calm voice. Stay on topic. Show respect, even when you disagree.	"I see it differently because . . ." "I respectfully disagree, and here's why . . ."
Build on Each Other's Ideas	Connect to what others say. Don't change the topic suddenly.	"I'd like to add to what ___ said . . ." "That reminds me of . . ."
Support Your Thinking	Use evidence or examples to explain your ideas.	"In the text it says . . ." "I believe this because . . ."
Ask Thoughtful Questions	Ask for clarification or input. Encourage others to speak.	"Can you explain more about that?" "What do others think?"
Include Everyone	Make space for all voices. Notice who hasn't spoken.	"Does anyone who hasn't spoken want to add something?" "Let's hear from someone new."
Stay Open-Minded	Be willing to rethink your ideas. Appreciate other views.	"I hadn't thought of it that way." "That makes me reconsider my idea."
Reflect and Grow	Think about what went well and what to improve.	"What did I learn?" "What could I do better next time?"

Common Classroom Applications

Elementary Examples

- **Start with a topic students want to explore.** Model using AI to provide basic information. Read the response and invite the class to talk with their peers about what they learned. Then ask for ideas to prompt the AI system further and share the results.

- **Engage in role-playing with AI.** Students ask the chatbot to take on the role of a character from a story they're reading and engage in a discussion as if they are talking with that character.

- **Have students submit their writing to AI and ask for ideas about improvement.** Then have students dialogue with AI about why the system recommended those improvements.

Secondary Examples

- **Require students to submit the transcripts of their interactions with AI.** Have them highlight their dialogue and the discussion stems that they use to interact with AI.
- **Use image generation to practice dialogue.** Students use an image generator and engage in dialogue to get the image closer to what they had in mind. Ask them to analyze the patterns of the dialogue and how the system responded.

Strategy in Action

One skill that is important in quality dialogue is argumentation. This requires that students can present, support, challenge, and refine their ideas using evidence and reasoning. These skills are useful in the context of AI because it turns the system into a thinking partner, rather than a source of information (one that many students simply accept as factual). Through argumentation, students are not simply consuming information. Rather, they are shaping it, questioning it, and engaging with it. There are several components to argumentation and sample sentence frames that build argumentation skills.

Making a claim	I observed _____ when _____.
	I compared _____ and _____.
	I noticed _____, when _____.
	The effect of _____ on _____ is _____.
Providing evidence	The evidence I use to support _____ is _____.
	I believe _____ (statement) because _____ (justification).
	I know that _____ is _____ because _____.
	Based on _____, I think _____.
	Based on _____, my hypothesis is _____.
Asking for evidence	I have a question about _____.
	Does _____ have more _____?
	What causes _____ to _____?
	Can you show me where you found the information about _____?

(Continued)

(Continued)		
Offering a counterclaim	I disagree _____ because _____. The reason I believe _____ is _____. The facts that support my idea are _____. In my opinion _____. One difference between my idea and yours is _____.	
Inviting speculation	I wonder what would happen if _____. I have a question about _____. I wonder why _____. What caused _____? How would this be different if _____? What do you think will happen if _____ next?	
Reaching consensus	I agree _____ because _____. How would this be different if _____? We all have the same idea about _____.	

Adapted from Ross, D., Fisher, D., & Frey, N. (2009). The art of argumentation. *Science and Children, 47*(3), p. 29.

Teacher Moves

- Use talk stems: "I agree with ___ because ___," "Can you explain what you mean by . . . ?"
- Model and role-play what dialogue looks like.
- Teach listening skills explicitly as they transfer to reading AI output.
- Provide video and audio examples of effective dialogue.
- Use graphic organizers to help track conversation threads or argument lines.

Student Moves

- Engage in partner and small group conversations, taking note of the ways that dialogue is used.
- Analyze their interactions with AI, noting the ways that they used dialogue and discussion guides to improve their output.
- Compare human and AI dialogue patterns. Students analyze how they use argumentation in conversations with classmates versus with AI.

DIALOGUE

> ## Extensions and Adaptations
>
> - **Advanced learners:** Engage students in AI Socratic debates. Have students pose a philosophical question or complex argument. Students analyze the AI's counterargument for logic, fallacies, and bias.
>
> - **Multilingual learners:** Encourage students to use AI as a language coach. Teach them to ask for help from their AI systems such as, "Can you say that again in another way?"
>
> - **Emerging readers:** Create interactive choice boards (e.g., cats or dogs, juice or milk) and have students make their choice and then ask AI to take the other perspective. Students can argue their perspective or discuss any valid points raised by AI.
>
> - **Cross-content:** Assign AI different roles and perspectives on a topic. This can include different historical perspectives, lived experiences, or philosophical ideologies. Students can analyze the output, synthesize perspectives, or develop a position statement.

Skill Progression by Grade Band

Grade Band	Skills	Supports
K–2: Practicing Simple Conversations and Listening Skills	• Engage in guided conversations with adults, peers, or AI using simple questions and responses • Use polite and respectful conversation stems (e.g., "I like . . . ," "Can you tell me more?") • Identify when an answer makes sense or doesn't with cue cards like thumbs up/thumbs down or a quantitative reflection • Learn different roles that are a part of strong conversations	• **Role-play activities to model turn-taking and polite responses** • Visual cues or sentence stems for initiating and responding • Student-friendly AI platforms for teacher modeling • Video clips or read-alouds that model clear, natural, and effective dialogue
3–5: Building Dialogue Skills for Clarification and Connection	• Understand how conversation partners respond by agreeing, disagreeing, or adding on • Ask follow-up questions to continue conversations with AI • Use respectful dialogue skills in peer and AI conversations • Track conversation threads and identify when more information is needed	• Sentence stems for different types of dialogue • Tool for tracking conversation and analyzing responses • **3-2-1 graphic organizers to help students prepare for discussion** • Collection of AI responses for practice identifying different types of successful dialogue

(Continued)

(Continued)

Grade Band	Skills	Supports
6–8: Developing Argumentation and Critical Dialogue Habits	• Engage in sustained, multi-turn conversations with AI and peers • Present claims and counterclaims using evidence • Ask for clarification or evidence from AI responses • Revise prompts and responses to improve the depth of dialogue	• Use argumentation frames and sentence starters • **Transcript of AI interactions for analysis of dialogue quality** • Tools to be used when highlights for different reasons (e.g., assumptions, counterpoints, clarification) • Models of effective feedback loops with AI
9–12: Leading and Analyzing High-Level Dialogue Across Domains	• Engage in Socratic-style dialogue with AI on abstract or ethical topics • Critically evaluate AI arguments for bias, depth, and logic • Use AI dialogue to synthesize multiple perspectives into a reasoned conclusion • Compare and contrast AI vs. human discourse for rhetorical effectiveness	• Transcripts of Socratic questioning and question stems for student analysis • Compare-contrast activity between AI dialogue and human dialogue • Chart that names situation, purpose, and type of dialogue needed • **Rubric for evaluating quality of dialogue and argumentation**

 Examples of the boldface supports above can be found on the book's companion website here: https://companion.corwin.com/courses/TeachingStudentsAI

Verification

WHAT IS IT?

Verification skills in learning involve the ability to critically evaluate information, sources, and one's own understanding for accuracy and reliability. These skills help students determine what is credible and accurate.

WHY IT MATTERS

Developing verification skills empowers learners to become independent thinkers and responsible consumers of information and is a critical dimension of information literacy. In an age of information overload, misinformation, and digital manipulation, these skills are essential for navigating complex media landscapes, making informed decisions, and engaging in civic discourse. When students learn to question sources and assess evidence, they are better equipped to participate thoughtfully in academic, social, and professional environments. This relevance extends beyond the classroom, preparing them for lifelong learning, consuming responsibly, and becoming developers of information in a rapidly evolving world.

HOW IT WORKS

"Spiders eat as much meat as all seven billion humans on the planet combined." Is that true or not? Middle school educators FitzHenry and Wilkens (2017) taught their students about verification skills using headlines like this, then gave their learners three minutes to locate credible sources that either supported or debunked the headline. Students then voted and shared the information they found, using guided discussion to whittle down the evidence. (It turns out that headline is true.) We checked another source to verify their claim: https://animals.howstuffworks.com/arachnids/spiders-eat-millions-tons-food-more-humans-annually. Although this was taught pre-AI, the skills remain the same.

The Civic Online Reasoning model (COR) was developed by the Stanford History Education Group as a frame for teaching students how to verify digital information they encounter (Wineburg et al., 2016-2020). The key components include

- **Lateral Reading.** Instead of staying on a site or chatbot, skilled readers open new queries to investigate the source (e.g., searching the organization or author) to determine credibility. This contrasts with vertical reading, where users stay on one page and try to evaluate from internal cues only.

- **Evaluating the Evidence.** Students are taught to question what kind of evidence supports a claim (data, expert opinion, primary source) and whether it's trustworthy.

- **Understanding the Source.** This includes examining the reputation, mission, and potential bias of a website, author, or publisher.
- **Corroboration.** Verify a claim by checking what other reliable sources say about the same topic.
- **Recognizing Sponsored Content and Manipulation.** Identifying native ads, clickbait, and other forms of media designed to persuade without transparency.

Common Classroom Applications

Elementary Examples

- **Compare human vs. AI information.** Present students with answers from an AI and a teacher-verified source (e.g., a textbook or child-friendly encyclopedia) and ask, "Are they the same? What's different? Which one do we trust and why?"
- **Use a simplified version of lateral reading.** Open a new tab and search the topic using a child-safe search engine like Kiddle or Google SafeSearch. Ask, "Do other sources say the same thing?"
- **Encourage peer verification.** Have peers discuss what they already know to be true about the topic and let students compare and verify AI-generated content together. Ask, "What do we already know?" or "Did we all get the same answer?"

Secondary Examples

- **Teach lateral reading explicitly.** Show students how to leave the original source or AI tool and open new tabs to search for the organization, author, or claim. Practice comparing multiple sources to verify AI-generated content.
- **Evaluate the source behind the AI.** Teach students to ask, "Where is this AI getting its information? Is it citing any sources? Are those sources credible?" Show them how some AI tools (like Bing Chat or Perplexity) cite sources, and some (like ChatGPT) do not by default.
- **Run trust tests on AI claims.** Provide students with AI-generated responses that are a mix of accurate and inaccurate statements. Ask students to
    - Identify the claim.
    - Research it independently.
    - Decide if it's credible.
    - Explain their process.

Strategy in Action

Integrating a verification protocol into student research projects is a powerful way to teach responsible AI use. When students use AI tools to gather information, they should be guided to verify each fact or claim before including it in their work. This begins with identifying specific pieces of information sourced from AI, such as statistics, historical events, or explanations of processes, and marking them for verification. For each claim, students confirm the accuracy by checking at least two credible and independent sources, such as academic databases, reputable news outlets, or official government and educational websites. They record their verification process in a simple log or source tracker, noting where and how they confirmed the information or whether it needed to be revised or removed due to inaccuracies. This practice builds strong research habits and helps students recognize the importance of using reliable sources. It also encourages them to think carefully about how they determine truth and accuracy.

Teacher Moves

- Promote curiosity and verification by asking, "How do you know that's true?"
- Encourage the use of multiple sources by requiring that they can verify at least two different sources.
- Connect misinformation (inaccurate information that was not deliberate) and disinformation (inaccurate information that is deliberate) to authentic consequences by asking, "What might happen if someone believed this and it wasn't true?"

Student Moves

- Set up peer reviews for fact-checking, allowing students to verify each other's independent sources.
- Create and use a verification checklist anchor chart and use it often. We like the questions proposed by Wineburg and colleagues (2016-2020): *Who's behind the information? What's the evidence? What do other sources say?*
- Encourage students to fact-check you. Fifth-grade teacher Scott Bedley (2017) notably wrote, "I taught my students how to spot fake news. Now they won't stop fact-checking me." Verification starts with us!

Extensions and Adaptations

- **Advanced learners:** Ask students to trace the origin of a claim to find the original study or dataset behind a widely cited fact or AI-generated claim.
- **Multilingual learners:** Set up multilingual "Fact-Check My Language!" stations using home-language websites (e.g., BBC Mundo, Deutsche Welle, ABS-CBN)

(Continued)

> (Continued)
>
> alongside English sources. Students verify claims or translations from AI using sources in both languages, then explain what they found in either language.
>
> - **Emerging readers:** Teach with visual examples using AI-generated images or content and compare with real photos or information to discuss. Ask students, "Does this look real?" and "What clues tell us it might be made up?"
>
> - **Cross-content:** Students examine math in the media by verifying statistical claims from news articles, social media posts, or AI outputs. In math, they analyze the accuracy of the numbers (percentages, averages, graphs), while in English they evaluate the clarity and fairness of the claims made using those statistics.

Skill Progression by Grade Band

Grade Band	Skills	Supports
K–2: Beginning Truth Detectives	<ul><li>Ask simple "Is it true?" questions</li><li>Notice differences between true and false claims</li><li>Recognize what makes a trusted source (e.g. adults, some books, certain websites)</li><li>Identify when something seems "made up" or wrong</li></ul>	<ul><li>Read-alouds options that have purposefully exaggerated or unrealistic content</li><li>**Visual cue cards to build early verification skills**</li><li>Sentence stems for pushing back and questioning during learning</li><li>Chart of what makes safe sources</li></ul>
3–5: Growing Information Investigators	<ul><li>Begin verifying simple facts using books and student-friendly websites</li><li>Identify source type (book, website, video)</li><li>Ask, "Where did this information come from?"</li><li>Detect obvious signs of bias or exaggeration</li></ul>	<ul><li>**Verification checklist and critical reading questions**</li><li>Graphic organizers for verification (e.g., fact-evidence-source)</li><li>Guidelines for safe search engines and platforms</li><li>Read-alouds (or video aloud) that have a reason for exaggeration</li></ul>
6–8: Developing Ethical Evaluators	<ul><li>Conduct lateral reading to verify AI-generated and online information</li><li>Distinguish between reliable and unreliable sources</li><li>Identify evidence that has been omitted in order to mislead</li><li>Cross-check facts across multiple sources</li><li>Reflect on why accurate information matters</li></ul>	<ul><li>**Lateral reading checklist for verifying content**</li><li>Source verification rubrics</li><li>Video mentors of a peer or teacher engaging in the verification process while learning</li><li>Graphic organizer designed for AI content analysis</li></ul>

VERIFICATION

Grade Band	Skills	Supports
9–12: Responsible Information Stewards	• Independently verify claims from multiple sources • Evaluate author expertise and intent • Recognize subtler forms of misinformation and disinformation • Understand the ethical implications of spreading false information	• Checklists for verification protocols • **Research prompts for practice with verification protocols** • Annotated bibliographies protocol for source verification • List of academic fact-checking tools and trusted databases

 Examples of the boldface supports above can be found on the book's companion website here: https://companion.corwin.com/courses/TeachingStudentsAI

Critical Interpretation

WHAT IS IT?

Critical interpretation is the ability to examine AI output beyond its surface meaning. To do so requires students to draw on a range of analytical, evaluative, and reasoning skills to determine whether the information is valid, useful, and appropriate for their purpose. When students regularly engage in this kind of analysis, they begin to approach AI not as an all-knowing tool, but as a collaborator whose output must be examined with care.

WHY IT MATTERS

Critical interpretation skills are essential for students engaging with AI-generated content, and teachers play a central role in helping students develop them. These skills matter because AI tools can produce information that appears fluent and authoritative, but may contain irrelevant tangents, flawed reasoning, or hidden assumptions. Without the ability to critically interpret output, students may accept incorrect information, overlook logical inconsistencies, or rely too heavily on surface-level responses.

HOW IT WORKS

Students need to develop the habit and disposition of asking whether the content is relevant to the task, purpose, and audience (Flower, 1990). This relevance filtering includes identifying off-topic information or overly broad answers that do not meet the specific goals of an assignment. They should further analyze the output for logical reasoning, such as asking whether the ideas are clearly connected, whether evidence supports the claims, and whether the argument holds together without contradictions.

Assumption identification is another crucial skill. Students should be taught to recognize when the AI relies on unstated beliefs, cultural norms, or dominant perspectives that may leave out alternative viewpoints (Gogoshin, 2025). In addition, students need to distinguish between surface-level responses that merely skim the topic and deeper, more thoughtful content that shows complexity and insight.

Common Classroom Applications

Elementary Examples

- **Teach what AI can and can't do.** Explain that AI doesn't "know" things; it also does not work like an encyclopedia. It predicts based on patterns and can be wrong. Use explanations such as, "AI is like a really fast guesser, but guessers need to be checked!"

- **"Can You Fool the Class?" verification challenge.** Have students write their own AI-style response (fact or fiction) and challenge classmates to verify the claim using sources.
- **Generate and analyze an informational text summary.** Students can use an AI tool to generate a summary of a short informational text they have already read and work in pairs to highlight the parts that are accurate and relevant and cross out anything that is incorrect or off topic. Once analyzed, they can jointly compose an improved version. They then revise the summary together using their own words and understanding, discussing how to make it clearer or more complete.

Secondary Examples

- **Discuss bias and limitations of AI.** Engage students in discussions about how AI tools reflect the data they're trained on, including biases in data, gaps in knowledge, and its limits on current events or regional content. Be explicit about how these limitations can potentially impact the topics you teach.
- **Perform relevance-filtering and accuracy checks.** Revise an AI-generated paragraph by comparing it to textbook explanations or other trusted primary and secondary sources. This activity provides practice with relevance filtering, accuracy checking, and using AI as a thinking partner rather than a shortcut.

Strategy in Action

Develop and utilize a four-step checklist of questions for students to regularly use as they analyze AI output that results from their queries. Students generate and submit their analysis along with the AI-generated content.

Step 1: Is it relevant?

- Does this answer actually help me with my question or task?
- Did the AI stay on topic, or does it go off in a different direction?
- Did it give too much or too little information for what I need?

Step 2: Does it make sense?

- Do the ideas connect in a clear and logical way?
- Does the explanation follow a step-by-step pattern I can follow?
- Is there anything that sounds confusing, mixed up, or out of order?

(Continued)

(Continued)

Step 3: What is it assuming?

- Does the response make a causal assumption about how something works, but does not explain it?
- Is the AI making general statements that might not be true for everyone?
- Are there hidden messages or opinions that I should question?

Step 4: Is it deep or just surface-level information?

- Is the answer just repeating basic facts, or is it explaining something in detail?
- Does it help me understand the "why" or "how," not just the "what"?
- Could I make this answer stronger by adding more thinking or examples?

Teacher Moves

- Model using think-alouds with an AI response you have generated, identifying strengths and weaknesses in the response. Be sure to explain why it is effective or not.
- Highlight strong and weak examples to compare relevance, clarity, and depth.
- Ask guiding questions taken from the checklist: "Does this make sense?" "What's missing?" "Does this give me enough information?"

Student Moves

- Underline useful, accurate information and cross out what's off topic or confusing.
- Annotate assumptions, missing perspectives, or logic gaps in AI output.
- Revise shallow responses to add explanation, reasoning, or multiple viewpoints.

Extensions and Adaptations

- **Advanced learners:** Invite students to compare outputs from two different AI tools or two different prompts and evaluate which one is more effective and why.
- **Multilingual learners:** Use structured graphic organizers that help students sort AI content into categories such as "on topic," "off topic," "fact," or "assumption."

> - **Emerging readers:** Read the AI output aloud together, stopping to ask guided questions such as, "Does this explain why?" or "Is this part important to the topic?" to develop reasoning and relevance filtering.
> - **Cross-content:** Have students evaluate whether the AI explanation of a concept is scientifically and historically accurate, complete, and reflective of current knowledge.

Skill Progression by Grade Band

Grade Band	Skills	Supports
K–2: Foundations of Sense-Making and Listening for Meaning	<ul><li>Listen to or read short AI responses and discuss what makes sense or doesn't</li><li>Sort content into categories like "on topic" or "not clear"</li><li>Identify one thing that helped them and one thing that was confusing</li><li>Ask questions like, "Is this part important?" or "Did this answer my question?"</li></ul>	<ul><li>Simplified AI-generated texts or visuals to support guided discussions</li><li>Sentence sorting activity for detailed vs. not detailed content</li><li>Read-alouds with student-facing guiding questions for interpretation</li><li>**Chart about assumption words like *always* or *best***</li></ul>
3–5: Beginning to Evaluate and Revise AI Output	<ul><li>Underline accurate or relevant information in AI responses</li><li>Cross out off-topic or confusing details</li><li>Revise shallow responses with more explanation or examples</li><li>Ask questions from a checklist: relevance, logic, assumptions, depth</li></ul>	<ul><li>**Critical interpretation checklist**</li><li>Think-alouds prompts for teachers to use when reading AI-generated content</li><li>Graphic organizers to sort content (fact/assumption, on/off topic)</li><li>Sentence frames for reflection (e.g., "This is helpful because . . . ")</li></ul>
6–8: Applying Reasoning and Detecting Assumptions	<ul><li>Critique AI responses for logical flow and missing reasoning</li><li>Identify unstated assumptions or dominant perspectives</li><li>Compare AI responses to known sources (textbook, article, etc.)</li><li>Revise or rewrite AI-generated text for clarity and depth</li></ul>	<ul><li>Think-aloud prompts for analyzing logic and reasoning</li><li>Discussion protocols for analyzing AI outputs</li><li>Tools for highlighting and annotating bias or logic flaws</li><li>**Activity that includes guided comparison of AI vs. human-written explanations**</li></ul>
9–12: Strategic Revision, Reflection, and Transfer	<ul><li>Engage in Socratic-style dialogue with AI on abstract or ethical topics</li><li>Critically evaluate AI arguments for bias, depth, and logic</li><li>Use AI dialogue to synthesize multiple perspectives into a reasoned conclusion</li><li>Compare and contrast AI vs. human discourse for rhetorical effectiveness</li></ul>	<ul><li>**Chart with examples of different types of discussions for analysis and discussion**</li><li>Prompts for analyzing AI–human dialogue</li><li>Tasks for practices with synthesizing positions from multiple AI roles or views</li><li>Rubrics for evaluating quality of dialogue and argumentation</li></ul>

 Examples of the boldface supports above can be found on the book's companion website here: https://companion.corwin.com/courses/TeachingStudentsAI

Curiosity

WHAT IS IT?

To build a strong sense of curiosity, students need to develop both cognitive skills and personal dispositions that support inquiry and exploration. Key skills include asking thoughtful questions, observing carefully, identifying patterns, making connections between new and prior knowledge, and tolerating ambiguity.

WHY IT MATTERS

Arguably, one of the greatest concerns educators have about the use of artificial intelligence in the classroom is that it can result in the uncurious creation of content (Brainard, 2025). AI should be used to support brainstorming, simulate perspectives, or gather ideas, but not to just generate a finished product. The dispositions that support curiosity include openness to new ideas, a willingness to wonder, and persistence in the face of uncertainty. Curiosity matters in learning because it drives intrinsic motivation and fosters deep engagement with the topic at hand. When students are curious, they are more likely to take ownership of their learning, pursue new knowledge independently, and sustain interest over time.

HOW IT WORKS

Curiosity is both trait-based and state-based. In other words, traits like inquisitiveness, imagination, and intellectual humility are all part of a curious mindset. As educators, we seek to create states in which curiosity can emerge and strengthen learning through sustained interaction. It turns out that, while counterintuitive, introducing uncertainty about a topic can create a learning state in which curiosity thrives. In other words, a well-placed "monkey wrench" in a task can create the necessary conditions for curiosity to thrive. For example, in one study, providing less-than-optimal information about a science task to make a motor work sparked deeper and more long-term learning because students used their curiosity to explore more options, eventually filling in the missing gaps, compared to those who had a well-defined, step-by-step list to complete the task (Lamnina & Chase, 2021). This confusion isn't a mistake; it's a deliberate strategy on the part of the teacher. The confounding variables introduced in the less well-defined task sparked curiosity and promoted inquiry by guiding students to realize that good scientific investigations require defining and isolating variables. That stands in contrast to too many "experiments" that are really just completing a series of tasks correctly to yield a predetermined outcome the teacher has already thought through.

Common Classroom Applications

Elementary Examples

- **Begin with a student-generated question or mystery related to your content.** Involve students in exploring or problem-solving. For example, model asking the chatbot a question that does not possess a clear "correct" answer. For example, ask, "What kind of creature could survive on a planet with lava oceans, ice storms, or no sunlight?" Then, show a strange real-world habitat (e.g., deep ocean vents).

- **Build background and introduce a curiosity-provoking question.** Show students extreme conditions on Earth, such as deep-sea vents on the bottom of the ocean, and then ask them to brainstorm their own imaginary planet or environment.

- **Introduce the uncertainty.** Use one or more of their imaginary environments and craft a prompt with them using descriptive language. Use AI (with guidance) and ask what adaptations living organisms would need to possess to survive. What would they eat? What shelter would they require?

- **Develop an infographic of your imaginary creature.** Students sketch, model, or build their creature out of craft materials or digitally.

Secondary Examples

- **Begin with a question that does not have a single answer.** How might the world be different if one major historical event had gone another way? For instance, you might ask, "What if we never landed on the moon?" or "What if Alexander Hamilton lived?" or "What if the internet had been invented in 1900?" This invites students to use their background knowledge to formulate responses, speculate, and investigate.

- **Introduce the uncertainty.** As students work to develop ideas, add a new wrinkle. Depending on the initial question, ask them to consider how this would have impacted art, technology, or daily life. They need to include real evidence to support their speculations.

- **Create a display to share with others.** Students create a poster of their event, an interview with another historical figure of the time, or a storyboard for a mini documentary of the imagined event.

Strategy in Action

Host The Museum of Unsolved Questions! What are the coolest things we still don't know about our world? Each student picks a mystery that fascinates them: Why do cats purr? What happened to Amelia Earhart? How long could humans live? Why do we dream?

Students can use the chatbot to gather what is currently known, the opinions of experts, and theories about their mystery. They then create a museum exhibit board or digital artifact with the question, what is known and unknown, and the uncertainty of what their own theory or next question to solve the mystery might be. You can then set up a curiosity boosting walk-through "museum" where other students leave sticky-note questions or ideas.

Teacher Moves

- Make space for curiosity breaks by setting aside 5–10 minutes for students to ask questions related to the lesson and explore them together or with AI support.

- Encourage divergent thinking by asking, "What are three different ways to explain this?" or "What might someone with a totally different perspective think?"

- Slow down the answer. Instead of jumping to the solution, spend time exploring the *why* or *how*. Delay closure with prompts such as, "Let's explore that idea more before we decide."

Student Moves

- Invite students to share interesting discoveries by bringing in curious facts, connections, or stories that relate to what you're learning.

- Create mystery or surprise by using mystery bags, blurred images, or story starters to build suspense.

- Develop question stems and language frames for students to use to challenge ideas respectfully ("Is there another way to think about this?") and build on other classmates' questions ("That makes me wonder about . . ." or "Can you talk more about that idea?").

Extensions and Adaptations

- **Advanced learners:** Make it global by inviting students to investigate how their question would be approached in different cultures or time periods.

- **Multilingual learners:** Use visuals and realia to anchor curiosity in images, videos, or physical objects that invite questioning without heavy text.

- **Emerging readers:** Use role-play or movement to explore big questions (e.g., "How do plants drink?" as a pantomime).
- **Cross-content:** After a hands-on investigation, have students write curiosity reports about something they still don't understand. These curiosity reports should address questions such as, "What surprised you? What new question do you have now?"

Skill Progression by Grade Band

Grade Band	Skills	Supports
K–2: Asking, Noticing, and Exploring	<ul><li>Ask simple "why" and "what" questions</li><li>Notice unusual or surprising things</li><li>Express curiosity through drawing or talking about learned topics</li><li>Think about bigger categories that a text or object is a part of and consider the "why"</li></ul>	<ul><li>Visuals or real objects that build curiosity</li><li>**Sentence stems for building curiosity**</li><li>Prompts for guided play and focused discovery</li><li>Read-aloud texts that promote speculation and lead to student questioning</li></ul>
3–5: Connecting and Questioning	<ul><li>Ask cause-and-effect or comparison questions</li><li>Group and refine related questions</li><li>Record questions and ideas in journals</li><li>Engage in structured inquiry and mini-research tasks</li></ul>	<ul><li>Graphic organizers for categorizing questions</li><li>Guided inquiry protocols</li><li>Discussion prompts based on different things to be curious about</li><li>**Chart that prompts ongoing and regular curiosity**</li></ul>
6–8: Deepening Inquiry and Perspective	<ul><li>Ask layered, open-ended, and speculative questions</li><li>Use reasoning and evidence to explore ideas</li><li>Challenge assumptions and consider multiple perspectives</li><li>Conduct extended self-directed investigations</li></ul>	<ul><li>List of digital tools and how they support different types of learning</li><li>**Templates for planning investigations of different topics**</li><li>Peer collaboration routines</li></ul>
9–12: Synthesizing, Reflecting, and Pursuing	<ul><li>Frame meaningful, researchable, and interdisciplinary questions</li><li>Sustain curiosity through long-term inquiry</li><li>Reflect on how and why their questions evolve</li></ul>	<ul><li>Options for independent passion-based projects that focus on AI sources</li><li>List of mentors, experts, or interview resources that can teach more information</li><li>**Tools for source evaluation and synthesis**</li></ul>

 Examples of the boldface supports above can be found on the book's companion website here: https://companion.corwin.com/courses/TeachingStudentsAI

Metacognition

WHAT IS IT?

Metacognition is the ability to think about your own thinking. It involves being aware of what you understand, noticing when you are confused, and choosing strategies to help yourself learn more effectively.

WHY IT MATTERS

Metacognitive skills are especially important when students are learning with AI because they help students take control of their learning instead of relying passively on technology. When students know how to plan their approach, monitor their understanding, and reflect on what they learn, they can use AI tools more effectively and responsibly. For example, they might evaluate whether an AI-generated answer makes sense, decide when to ask for more information, or recognize when they need to try a different strategy. These skills help students become thoughtful users of AI, not just consumers of quick answers, and support deeper, more meaningful learning.

HOW IT WORKS

Metacognitive skills include the ability to plan, monitor, and evaluate one's own thinking and learning. These skills help students set goals, choose effective strategies, recognize when they are confused, and adjust as needed. When students use AI tools in the classroom, metacognition becomes especially important because technology often offers multiple paths, suggestions, or feedback. Without metacognitive awareness, students may accept AI-generated responses without questioning their accuracy, relevance, or depth.

Research by Flavell (1979), who introduced the concept of metacognition, and later studies by Schraw and Dennison (1994) highlight that students who develop strong metacognitive skills tend to perform better academically and engage more deeply with content. In AI-supported learning, this means students need to assess when and how to use AI, whether the information is useful, and how to respond to it thoughtfully. For example, a student using an AI writing assistant should be able to decide which suggestions improve clarity and which might weaken their argument. As AI becomes more integrated into classrooms, metacognitive skills act as a safeguard, helping students remain critical thinkers and active learners. Supporting students in developing these skills ensures that AI is used not just as a shortcut, but as a tool for deeper learning and self-directed growth. Yang and Xia (2023), in their investigation of the influence of AI on student metacognition, identified these skills as being especially important for making the most of these experiences:

- **Self-assessment and reflection.** Students think about what they understand, what they need to improve, and how AI helped or didn't help their learning.
- **Learning strategy selection.** Students choose which tools, prompts, or supports within the AI system best match the kind of task they are working on.
- **Learning plans and goal setting.** Students set clear learning goals and decide how they will use AI to support those goals during a task or over time.
- **Learning process monitoring.** Students keep track of their progress while using AI, noticing when they are improving, getting stuck, or need to try a new approach.
- **Situational cognitive adaptation.** Students adjust their thinking or strategies based on how the AI responds, what the task demands, or how the situation changes.
- **Recognition and response to learning barriers.** Students notice when they don't understand something or when AI isn't helping, and take action to get back on track, such as asking for clarification or switching strategies.

Common Classroom Applications

Elementary Examples

- **Promote self-assessment and reflection.** After completing an activity using an AI tool (like a reading assistant or platform such as Khanmigo), have students fill out a simple reflection sheet with prompts such as, What did I learn today? What was tricky? Did the AI help me or confuse me?

- **Teach students how to use learning intentions and success criteria in their prompts.** Build the habit of starting the session by including both. For example, "Today I am learning about the Milky Way galaxy. My success criteria are to be able to describe how it was formed and its features. Help me be successful as I ask you questions!"

- **Build in pause points so they can monitor their progress.** Have partners check in with each other to discuss, "Is this working? Do I understand what the chatbot is showing me?" Make sure there are processes in place for students to seek help from you to clear up confusions.

Secondary Examples

- **Require students to plan, not just dive in.** Before using an AI tool, students review a strategy menu and select an approach that matches the task (e.g., using AI to brainstorm, revise, or critique). Add metacognitive pause points in lessons where students explain their tool selection during class discussions. Afterward, they justify their choice and evaluate its effectiveness.

(Continued)

(Continued)

- **Structure some tasks to promote situational cognitive adaptation.** Provide scenarios related to the topic being taught where the chatbot has given a misleading, incomplete, or overly simple response. Students must adapt by rephrasing, seeking other sources, or combining AI input with critical reasoning. Ask them reflective questions about how they responded: "How did you adjust when AI gave you a vague or incorrect answer? What did you do when the chatbot wasn't helpful?"

- **Heighten their awareness of recognizing and responding to learning barriers.** Teach students to identify AI-related learning obstacles (e.g., overreliance, vague answers, confirmation bias) and respond with strategies such as asking clarifying questions, cross-referencing with a trusted source, or switching to human collaboration. Use case studies or "AI fails" as discussion starters to analyze how students might respond in similar situations.

Strategy in Action

Self-assessment can play a powerful role in helping students become more metacognitively aware of their thinking. When students reflect on their learning process while using AI, rather than just the product, they develop awareness of how and when AI supports or limits their understanding. Provide students with a structured self-assessment checklist to use before, during, and after their work. This might include items such as

"I used AI to help me . . . "

"One suggestion I accepted was _____ because _____."

"I still need to learn more about . . . "

Over time, students learn to pause, evaluate their own use of AI, and make decisions about when to rely on it and when to challenge or supplement it. This turns AI into a learning partner rather than a shortcut. Here is one example of an AI self-assessment checklist you can use or revise for your own students.

Before I Start Chatting:
- Do I know what I want to learn or figure out?
- Did I think of a clear question to ask?
- Am I ready to learn something new?

While I'm Chatting:

- Am I reading the chatbot's answers carefully?
- Am I asking follow-up questions if I don't understand?
- Am I thinking about how this connects to what I already know?

After the Chat:

- Did I learn something new or useful?
- Can I explain what I learned in my own words?
- What will I do next with this information?

Teacher Moves

- Model thinking aloud to verbalize how you engage in planning, monitoring, and adjusting your own learning during a task.
- Teach specific learning strategies so students can build a toolkit of approaches for how to help themselves when they get stuck (e.g., rereading, chunking, questioning) and explain when to use them.
- Ask students, "What's one thing you were confused about and how did you deal with it?" to promote recognition of learning barriers and self-correction.

Student Moves

- Create student learning journals or logs so students can track what strategies they tried, how they worked, and what they learned about themselves as learners.
- Use rubrics that include process success criteria, not just product success criteria.
- Create peer talk routines like, "Ask your partner what strategy they're using" to support metacognitive conversations.

Extensions and Adaptations

- **Advanced learners:** Let students be metacognitive coaches by writing short tips for peers about how to stay in charge of their thinking when working with AI, based on their own learning experiences.
- **Multilingual learners:** Provide prompt reflection cards with questions like, "What did I ask AI?" and "What will I do next?" to guide real-time monitoring in the supported language.

(Continued)

> (Continued)
> - **Emerging readers:** Use the voice-to-text feature, available on most AI platforms, to allow students to record spoken reflections (e.g., "The chatbot helped me because . . . " or "Next time I will . . . ").
> - **Cross-content:** After working with AI in one subject (e.g., using AI to help write a science explanation), students are asked to use the same thinking strategy (e.g., question generation or self-explanations) in a completely different domain (e.g., analyzing historical causes). Students can then reflect on how their strategy use changed and whether it transferred effectively.

Skill Progression by Grade Band

Grade Band	Skills	Supports
K–2: Learning to Notice My Thinking	• Recognize when help is needed and identify what some of the things are that should come next • Describe what they are working on and why it matters • Reflect with support on what they learned and how they felt	• Teacher think-aloud prompts that support metacognition • **Thinking about thinking organizer and tool** • Guided discussion and story-based reflection • Simple sentence starters (e.g., "I tried . . . " or "Next time I will . . . ")
3–5: Becoming a Reflective Learner	• Sets simple goals for a task • Chooses a strategy and explains why they used it • Monitors progress and identifies when they are confused • Reflects on what helped or didn't help • Identifies what they would do differently next time	• Graphic organizers for strategy tracking • Goal-setting checklists and journals • **Partner talk protocols for metacognitive discussion** • Mid-task and end-of-task reflection routines
6–8: Managing My Own Learning	• Plans how to approach complex tasks, especially those that extend for several days • Monitors understanding and adapts strategies when needed • Describes how a specific strategy supported learning • Reflects on successes and challenges in learning process • Sets goals for how to improve strategy use in the future	• Strategy menus and planning tools • Templates for independent learning logs and work plans • Independent learning logs or journals • **Student-facing reflection and teacher feedback tool** • Peer-feedback protocols focused on process, not just product

METACOGNITION

Grade Band	Skills	Supports
9–12: Taking Ownership of Learning	• Independently selects and adapts strategies across contexts • Evaluates the effectiveness of strategies after tasks • Reflects on patterns in their learning over time • Sets personal learning goals (not just those set by the teacher) and tracks progress toward them • Transfers metacognitive strategies across disciplines	• Advanced reflection tools for metacognitive thinking • Protocols for peer-led metacognitive debriefings • **Chart of options for strategy transfer** • Long-term goal-tracking systems (e.g., digital portfolios)

 Examples of the boldface supports above can be found on the book's companion website here: https://companion.corwin.com/courses/TeachingStudentsAI

Cognitive Flexibility

WHAT IS IT?

Cognitive flexibility is the ability to shift thinking between different concepts, adapt to new information, and approach problems from multiple perspectives. In the classroom, it helps students adjust their learning strategies when facing challenges, make connections across subjects, and respond effectively to changes in tasks or instructions.

WHY IT MATTERS

Developing cognitive flexibility in students is essential because it equips learners to navigate complex and changing classroom demands with resilience, adaptability, and curiosity (Spiro et al., 1988). Students with strong cognitive flexibility can shift their thinking when they encounter new ideas, reconsider their assumptions, and adapt their strategies when a task becomes more difficult or unfamiliar. This ability not only strengthens their problem-solving and critical thinking skills but also enhances their capacity to learn from errors, engage in meaningful discussions, and transfer their learning across different subjects and contexts. Promoting the development of cognitive flexibility in students means fostering a learning environment where they feel safe to explore multiple solutions, ask questions, and reflect on their learning process.

HOW IT WORKS

Cognitive flexibility is both impacted by and increasingly important in the age of AI. On one hand, AI tools can support cognitive flexibility by exposing students to diverse perspectives, generating multiple approaches to a problem, and offering adaptive feedback that encourages learners to shift their thinking (Chauncey & McKenna, 2023). For example, when students use AI to explore various interpretations of a text or test different problem-solving strategies, they are practicing the skill of switching mental sets and adapting to new information. AI can also personalize learning paths, prompting students to make decisions, adjust strategies, and reflect on their choices, which are key aspects of cognitive flexibility.

On the other hand, overreliance on AI without critical thinking can hinder cognitive flexibility. If students passively accept AI-generated outputs without questioning or evaluating them, they may miss opportunities to develop more flexible thinking. That's why cognitive flexibility is a crucial trait when using AI. Students must be able to assess the credibility, relevance, and limitations of AI-generated content, decide when and how to use AI tools, and adapt their learning strategies accordingly. For example, studies in AI-based adaptive learning systems show that such tools can foster flexible thinking by prompting learners to adjust their responses based on feedback and encounter multiple solution paths (Holmes et al., 2019). However, the benefit depends on the learner's ability to engage reflectively and not just follow AI recommendations without question.

> ## Common Classroom Applications
>
> ### Elementary Examples
>
> - **Ask wonder questions with AI helpers.** Let students ask big, open-ended questions related to the topic being taught ("Why do animals migrate?") then use an AI tool to explore different answers. They can compare what the AI says with what they already know or what their classmates think, helping them see ideas in new ways.
>
> - **Use "What If?" story starters.** Students ask AI to help create fun "what if" scenarios ("What would a day without numbers be like?" or "What if the moon were made of marshmallows?") then write or draw their own endings. This helps them imagine different outcomes and think flexibly.
>
> - **Fix-it activities.** Students enter a sentence or math problem into the chatbot and ask it to help fix a mistake. They then explain what was wrong and what they learned, turning errors into learning moments.
>
> ### Secondary Examples
>
> - **Debate and perspective-taking with AI role-play.** Students prompt the chatbot to take on different viewpoints (e.g., historical figures or stakeholders) in a debate, then must interact with and challenge these AI personas, developing perspective-shifting skills.
>
> - **Project planning and AI collaboration.** Students use AI collaboratively in small groups to plan a multi-day project, requiring them to negotiate roles, merge ideas, and adapt to new group dynamics and tool interactions.
>
> - **AI-supported problem-solving in math and science.** Students solve problems on their own, then ask the chatbot for alternative methods or explanations, comparing and analyzing different approaches to strengthen flexible problem-solving.

> ## Strategy in Action
>
> Adaptive learning programs are widely used in classrooms, but do not reach their potential when teachers assign them without fostering the critical thinking and cognitive flexibility that are necessary to fuel learning. Too often we have
>
> *(Continued)*

(Continued)

seen students simply going through the motions of using an adaptive learning program, essentially reducing them to digital worksheets. Teach about cognitive flexibility to heighten their awareness of what occurs in the program and watch for signs that students are (or are not) fully engaging. Here's a student-friendly list of thinking strategies that promote cognitive flexibility when using adaptive learning programs:

- **Try New Ways When Something Doesn't Work.** If your first strategy doesn't work, don't give up. Try a different way! These programs want to see how flexible your thinking is.

- **Be Ready for New Ideas.** The program might teach you something you haven't seen before. Stay open and curious, even if it feels tricky at first.

- **Learn From Mistakes.** Don't just click "Next." Read why something was wrong, and ask yourself, "What can I do differently next time?"

- **Use What You Already Know in New Ways.** Watch for how today's lesson connects to something you've already learned. Can you use an old skill to help with this new challenge?

- **Pick the Right Help When You Need It.** If the program offers hints or videos, think about which one will help you the most, not just the fastest.

- **Notice When You Need to Slow Down or Speed Up.** Pay attention to your pace. Are you rushing and making mistakes? Or stuck and need a break or a new plan?

- **Watch for Changes in the Task.** Sometimes the questions or directions change. Stay alert! Ask yourself, "Is this the same kind of problem, or is it asking me to think differently?"

- **Balance Speed and Accuracy.** It's great to be fast, but only if you're also being careful. Find a rhythm that works for *you*.

Teacher Moves

- Promote transfer of learning by asking, "Can you connect this to something we learned before?"

- Use Think-Compare-Share by asking students to first think individually, then compare different methods or answers before sharing.

- Spark exploration of multiple strategies by asking, "What's another way to solve this?"

Student Moves

- Introduce language frames that foster cognitive flexibility, such as, "I used to think _____, but now I think _____." or "This strategy worked better because ___."
- On "Two Ways Tuesday" ask students to solve each problem two different ways and compare.
- Add peer discussion roles like Strategy Explorer or Perspective Builder during collaborative group work.

Extensions and Adaptations

- **Advanced learners:** Give students an AI-generated answer or text and challenge them to reverse-engineer the response by creating possible prompts that could have led to it.
- **Multilingual learners:** Use AI in two languages to generate answers in their home language and English, then compare vocabulary, phrasing, and meaning shifts.
- **Emerging readers:** Use AI-generated word ladders (change one sound to make a new word) to help students think flexibly about sound-letter correspondence.
- **Cross-content:** Use the chatbot as a music mood generator to describe how different types of music might affect focus or feelings during work, then let students try different styles during learning tasks and reflect on their adaptability.

Skill Progression by Grade Band

Grade Band	Skills	Supports
K–2: Learning to Shift	• Try different strategies when something doesn't work • Follow changing rules in games or classroom routines • Retell stories in new ways or change endings • Recognize and describe different feelings or ideas	• Visual cues (charts, icons) to signal shifts • Structured choice (e.g., two solution options) • **"What if?" storytelling game** • Activities focused on rule-shifting (e.g., Red-Light, Green-Light, Simon Says, Category Shift) • Think-aloud prompts for teacher modeling of cognitive thinking

(Continued)

(Continued)

Grade Band	Skills	Supports
3–5: Flexible Thinkers at Work	• Compare different approaches to a task • Reflect and revise based on feedback • Consider another student's perspective or strategy • Explain one idea in multiple ways • Connect learning across subjects	• **Ways to be a flexible thinker anchor chart** • Peer discussion routines (Turn-and-Try) • Graphic organizers and multi-modal output options • Self-assessment tools for cognitive flexibility
6–8: Adapting and Applying	• Shift thinking when faced with conflicting or new information • Apply prior knowledge to new or unfamiliar problems • Switch strategies when one isn't effective • Engage in perspective-taking in writing and discussion • Integrate feedback from multiple sources (peers, teacher, AI)	• Problem-based learning scenarios • Transcripts of Socratic seminars and debates that highlight cognitive flexibility • Revision protocols for getting feedback from multiple sources • **Flexible thinking with AI support student-facing chart**
9–12: Thinking Across Boundaries	• Evaluate and select among multiple strategies or viewpoints • Adapt communication for different audiences or formats • Reframe problems and generate alternative solutions	• **Advanced writing tasks with audience/purpose shifts** • Prompts to explore, test, and refine thinking when using AI • Rubrics that assess strategy use and adaptability • Timeline-style tool for tracking thinking

 Examples of the boldface supports above can be found on the book's companion website here: https://companion.corwin.com/courses/TeachingStudentsAI

Ethical Reasoning

WHAT IS IT?

Ethical reasoning skills for student use with AI involve the ability to recognize and evaluate the moral implications of using artificial intelligence in learning and daily life. Students use these skills to consider fairness, privacy, bias, and responsibility when interacting with AI tools, ensuring their choices align with ethical and respectful practices.

WHY IT MATTERS

Ethical reasoning skills are essential when students use AI because they support thoughtful and responsible decision-making. These skills help students move beyond simply asking, "Can we use this tool?" to thoughtfully considering, "Should we use this tool, and in what ways?" Ethical reasoning encourages students to examine the potential impacts of AI, including fairness, bias, and privacy, and to make choices that reflect integrity and respect for others. This approach helps prepare students to be both informed users and responsible contributors in a world shaped by artificial intelligence. Young people of all ages draw on empathy, critical thinking, and respect for others to make decisions about dilemmas that arise in their academic and social lives.

HOW IT WORKS

Ethical reasoning develops over time and is shaped by a child's cognitive and emotional growth. Young children typically understand ethics through concepts like fairness and sharing (Hedefalk & Sumpter, 2025). As they move into adolescence, their reasoning becomes more complex, incorporating personal beliefs, loyalty, and values that extend beyond rules and consequences. This progression presents a challenge for educators who must support students in navigating increasingly nuanced ethical decisions. Research in digital citizenship and media literacy underscores the importance of critical thinking in evaluating technology's influence on learning and society. In a digital world where algorithms tailor content to reinforce users' existing values and beliefs, young people are especially at risk of becoming trapped in echo chambers that limit exposure to diverse perspectives and restrict intellectual growth (Hobbs, 2020).

Common Classroom Applications

Elementary Examples

- **Use read-alouds and stories with dilemmas.** Select books or short stories that explore dilemmas, including those that explore digital or AI-related themes (e.g., a robot learning right from wrong). Ask students to consider what makes a decision ethical when humans and technology are involved.

- **Teach the language of digital ethics.** Introduce vocabulary like *privacy*, *fairness*, *responsibility*, *respect for digital work*, and *truthfulness online*. Create a word wall that links traditional ethical terms to digital and AI contexts.

- **Host digital circle discussions.** Use classroom meetings to discuss digital behavior: "Should we always trust what AI says?" or "What if AI gives different answers to different people?"

Secondary Examples

- **Analyze AI case studies in the news.** Use age-relevant stories about AI use in hiring, policing, or health care. Ask students to identify stakeholders, ethical dilemmas, and consequences, and prompt discussion by asking, "What's fair?" "What's right?" and "Who benefits and who does not?"

- **Teach and use an ethical decision-making frame.** Provide a tool like the SHOULD model and utilize it in the context of your content or subject:
    - Situation: What is happening?
    - Harms: Who could be harmed?
    - Options: What are the possible actions?
    - Universal values: What's fair, just, and respectful?
    - Long-term impact: What could happen in the future?
    - Decision: What is the most ethical choice?

- **Engage families and communities.** Assign home conversations or intergenerational interviews to learn how adults use or worry about AI in their lives. Host a student-led forum to discuss their findings and their points of agreement or disagreement.

Strategy in Action

Role-playing tech scenarios is a powerful way to engage students in ethical reasoning by placing them in realistic, age-appropriate situations where they must make thoughtful decisions involving AI. For example, students might act out a scene in which a classmate uses an AI writing tool to complete a group project without telling others, prompting discussion about honesty, transparency, and fairness. Another scenario could involve a student using a chatbot to answer questions during a test, raising questions about academic integrity and responsible use. After acting out the scenarios, students reflect as a class on the choices made, the consequences of those choices, and how ethical principles such as respect, responsibility, and justice apply. This strategy allows students to explore complex issues in a safe, supported environment while developing empathy and critical thinking skills that prepare them for real-life digital dilemmas.

Teacher Moves

- Pose open-ended ethical questions when teaching content such as, "What's the right thing to do?" or "Who might be affected by this choice?"

- Use wait time to support deeper thinking to give students time to reflect before answering ethical dilemmas. Allowing for silent processing or written reflection before discussion provides students with the opportunity to think beyond a superficial answer.

- Normalize uncertainty and reinforce that ethical reasoning often involves complex, unclear answers. Encourage learners to revisit and revise their thinking as they gather more information.

Student Moves

- Provide a decision-making tree visual tool for students to walk through a complex decision step by step. It can include prompts like, "What are my choices? Who will this affect? What are the short- and long-term consequences?"

- Create media literacy fact-checking opportunities using AI-generated or online content. Have students verify claims, check sources, and assess fairness, then tie this activity to discussions on misinformation and the ethical use of information.

- Use ethical exit tickets at the end of a lesson that ask students to respond to a short prompt such as, "How might today's topic relate to doing the right thing?"

Extensions and Adaptations

- **Advanced learners:** Ask students to reflect on ethical shifts over time and how it has changed on some topics (e.g., civil rights, environmental responsibility, the right of women and people of color to vote).

(Continued)

> (Continued)
>
> - **Multilingual learners:** Encourage students to share how values are taught in their families or cultures when discussing universal themes of fairness, truth, or kindness.
> - **Emerging readers:** Use conflicts to guide reflection on everyday classroom issues (e.g., turn-taking, hurt feelings) using respectful, structured conversations.
> - **Cross-content:** Analyze digital citizenship issues like privacy, plagiarism, or AI responsibility using media examples and ethical frameworks, and closely examine how statistical information is used ethically and accurately.

Skill Progression by Grade Band

Grade Band	Skills	Supports
K–2: Recognizing Right and Wrong	• Identify fair vs. unfair behavior • Express feelings about actions • Recognize how actions affect others • Begin to take others' perspectives	• **Picture books with clear ethical messages** • Role-play scenarios that focus on making ethical decisions • Sentence stems for ethical thinking ("That was fair because . . . ") • If . . . Then . . . style protocol for decision-making
3–5: Considering Consequences and Fairness	• Predict consequences of actions • Discuss fairness and justice in simple scenarios • Compare different points of view • Begin to recognize ethical dilemmas	• Prompts for structured debates on applicable ethical topics • Discussion protocols to engage in ethical thinking • Books or topics designed for group reading or study • **Practicing values in a digital world classroom chart**
6–8: Analyzing Multiple Perspectives	• Analyze motives and outcomes • Consider cultural, social, and emotional contexts • Evaluate conflicting values in dilemmas • Reflect on personal values and beliefs	• Case studies and current AI-related events • Prompts for ethical reflection • Group discussion (and debate) structures for ethical reasoning • **Discussion and debate structures for ethical reasoning**

ETHICAL REASONING

Grade Band	Skills	Supports
9–12: Synthesizing and Justifying Ethical Decisions	• Formulate and defend ethical positions • Apply ethical frameworks (e.g., ethics of care, rights-based, common good) • Explore the ethical dimensions of complex systems • Reflect on ethical development and civic responsibility	• Collection of texts that address issues with AI use • **Checklists for ethical vs. nonethical learning behaviors** • Independent project prompts that explore subject-related ethical issues • Place for students to comfortably share ethical questions they have while learning

 Examples of the boldface supports above can be found on the book's companion website here: https://companion.corwin.com/courses/TeachingStudentsAI

Self-Regulation

WHAT IS IT?

Self-regulation is the ability of learners to manage their thoughts, emotions, and behaviors to achieve personal learning goals. Cognitively, it involves setting goals, sustaining attention, and reflecting on progress; emotionally, it includes recognizing feelings, managing frustration, and maintaining motivation during the learning process.

WHY IT MATTERS

Self-regulation is essential for learning because it empowers students to take ownership of their educational journey. These skills help learners persist through difficulty, adapt strategies when needed, and remain motivated, especially in complex or self-directed tasks. While AI can support the development of cognitive self-regulation by offering feedback, scaffolds, and personalized reminders, it is not well-equipped to detect or respond to the nuanced emotional states of learners, such as subtle shifts in motivation or anxiety. AI also cannot replace the relational and contextual guidance provided by teachers, who can model self-regulation, build trust, and create environments where learners feel safe to take risks and reflect deeply. Ultimately, developing self-regulation requires both internal growth and supportive human interactions that AI alone cannot fully provide.

HOW IT WORKS

Self-directed learning (SDL) skills are essential when using AI tools because they help students engage with these technologies in thoughtful and effective ways. SDL includes setting learning goals, selecting strategies, monitoring progress, and adjusting actions based on feedback. These skills are especially important when interacting with AI, as students must decide what questions to ask, how to evaluate the responses they receive, and when to seek additional information or support. Research supports the value of SDL in technology-rich learning environments (Lee & Chang, 2025), showing that students with strong self-direction are more likely to use digital tools to build deep understanding. But without these skills, students may use AI passively, accept inaccurate answers, or miss opportunities to extend their learning. Developing SDL in face-to-face environments ensures that learners remain active thinkers and decision-makers when working with advanced technologies (Lee et al., 2014).

While cognitive and metacognitive skills are crucial for self-directed learning (e.g., planning, staying on track), so are emotional skills. Emotion and motivation are the fire under cognition. They ignite learning. Yeager (2024), who writes about motivation of children, adolescents, and young adults, notes that "emotion is a learning tool. It teaches you what to retreat from and what to approach; that's why it is so important in establishing that emotions are not secondary to the reasoning parts of the brain" (p. 43). These skills include the following:

- **Help-Seeking.** Knowing when and how to seek support from peers, teachers, or digital resources when needed.
- **Motivation and Persistence.** Maintaining focus, managing frustration, and staying committed to long-term learning goals.
- **Self-Motivation and Interest Management.** Finding personal relevance in tasks and sustaining engagement, even when challenges arise.

Common Classroom Applications

Elementary Examples

- **Normalize help-seeking.** Create a help menu in the classroom with steps like, "Ask yourself," "Check your notes," "Ask a classmate," and "Ask the teacher." Be sure to reinforce when students seek help and offer help to others.

- **Use AI to foster motivation and persistence.** Set personal learning goals with students and revisit them frequently so they can monitor progress and celebrate successes. AI chat tools can prompt students with sentence starters or question scaffolds like, "What do you want to get better at in reading?" or "What's one thing you want to finish by Friday?" You can also automate reminders to send personalized nudges like, "You planned to finish your story by today. How's it going?" or "Remember your goal to ask one good question during science."

- **Foster self-motivation and interest management by providing choice.** Choice is related to topics, formats, or projects that boost ownership and relevance. Remember that when you offer choice, you are also teaching decision-making, a key to cognitive self-regulation skills.

Secondary Examples

- **Elevate help-seeking as a key to success.** Teach and model the difference between productive struggle and when it's time to ask for help. Encourage students to develop and use a personalized list of trusted academic resources (e.g., textbooks, online databases, peer mentors).

- **Teach students how to create individualized study schedules or to-do lists with the help of AI planning tools.** Students can input available time, due dates, and personal goals, and AI can generate a weekly or daily study plan. The chatbot can also take a long-term assignment (e.g., "Write a research paper due in three weeks") and help break it into smaller steps like topic selection, outline creation, research, drafting, revision, and final edits.

- **Use AI to brainstorm based on personal interests and knowledge.** Ask the chatbot to reframe content in relatable contexts (e.g., "Explain the Cold War in terms of Marvel superheroes"). After all, learning is always about going from the known to the new.

Strategy in Action

When students are assigned a science project due in a few weeks, they often feel overwhelmed by the scope and timeline. To build self-directed learning and self-regulation skills, teachers can guide students in breaking the project into manageable phases, such as choosing a topic, designing the experiment, collecting data, analyzing results, and preparing a display. AI tools can support this process by helping students generate personalized study plans based on their schedules and pacing preferences.

In the early days, AI can suggest topics, help students refine testable questions, and model how to write a hypothesis. As students move into experimentation, the chatbot can provide step-by-step guidance for data collection and analysis, offer sample charts, or explain unfamiliar math. In the final phase, AI can assist with drafting conclusions and designing presentation materials, all aligned with the assigned rubric.

If a student falls behind, AI can revise the plan to help redistribute the remaining tasks. The teacher, of course, is a crucial player throughout, monitoring how well students use their plans, reflect on progress, and seek help when needed. This approach transforms a complex assignment into a series of clear, achievable steps, while supporting students in developing independence, time management, and effective learning habits.

Teacher Moves

- Build problem-solving skills by asking, "Who or what could you use to help you solve this?"
- Links tasks to interests by asking, "What part of this connects to something you care about?"
- Highlight examples of persistence and problem-solving, and celebrate effort and improvement, not just completion.

Student Moves

- Build AI into planning by having students use it to break down larger assignments into smaller, manageable steps.
- Teach students to use motivational prompts when the work gets frustrating. For instance, ask the chatbot, "Give me three reasons not to give up on this project."
- Show students how they can prompt the chatbot to generate flashcards, vocabulary lists, and concept maps to build the habit of study.

> **Extensions and Adaptations**
>
> - **Advanced learners:** Challenge students to analyze when not to rely on AI help and justify their decisions. For example, when is peer feedback better than AI?
> - **Multilingual learners:** Use AI to help script help-seeking phrases in English. "How do I politely ask my teacher to repeat something I didn't understand?"
> - **Emerging readers:** Ask AI to generate choice boards or menus based on student interests using images and simple text.
> - **Cross-content:** Ask the chatbot to track frustration or engagement across subjects. "I get stuck in science more than in art. Why do you think that is?"

Skill Progression by Grade Band

Grade Band	Skills	Supports
K–2: Beginning Self-Managers	• Recognizes when they need help • Expresses basic emotions related to learning • Tries again after mistakes	• Visual cue cards for students to use as a part of self-regulation • **"What to do if . . . " coaching tool for self-regulation** • Emotion check-ins with icons or puppets • Tools that show the ways to ask for help
3–5: Emerging Independent Learners	• Asks for help using appropriate language • Identifies strategies that help them stay focused • Sets simple goals • Manages frustration during challenging tasks	• **Sentence stems to use when help-seeking from self, peers, or teachers** • Daily goal-setting templates on self-regulation • Chart that names "What to do when . . . " solutions to common frustrations when learning
6–8: Developing Strategic Learners	• Monitors progress and adjusts plans • Chooses strategies for staying motivated • Identifies emotional triggers and uses coping strategies • Seeks help from a range of sources (peer, teacher, AI)	• Digital planners for organizing tasks and tracking goals • **Menu of self-regulation strategies** • Student-facing and student-created If . . . Then . . . chart for self-regulation
9–12: Self-Directed Learners	• Sets long-term learning goals • Evaluates when and how to seek help • Manages complex emotions like stress or boredom • Sustains motivation through self-generated interest connections	• AI tools designed to assist with planning and reflection • Personalized goal-tracking dashboards • Checklist for emotional awareness when learning • **AI prompts to help find relevance in topics and tasks**

 Examples of the boldface supports above can be found on the book's companion website here: https://companion.corwin.com/courses/TeachingStudentsAI

Teacher Decision-Making: When Students Can Use AI (and When They Cannot)

WHAT IS IT?

Every day, teachers make countless decisions that shape how learning unfolds in their classrooms—including when to allow or limit students' use of AI tools. These choices are not just about managing technology; they reflect deeper beliefs about learning, equity, and academic integrity.

WHY IT MATTERS

The way teachers manage student access to AI directly influences how students develop critical thinking, creativity, and problem-solving skills in a world shaped by emerging technologies. When AI tools are used without clear guidance, they can replace meaningful cognitive effort with convenience. This may lead to shallow learning, mask students' understanding, and widen existing achievement gaps. At the same time, overly strict or inconsistent restrictions can limit students' opportunities to learn how to use AI in responsible and thoughtful ways. These decisions reflect deeper values about what counts as learning, who has access to powerful tools, and how teachers balance support with challenge. Teacher decision-making, even in small moments, helps shape classrooms that are both fair and future-ready.

HOW IT WORKS

As AI becomes increasingly integrated into educational settings, teachers are encountering complex dilemmas regarding student access to AI tools. A significant concern is the potential for students to over-rely on AI, which may impede the development of critical cognitive skills. A systematic review of the research on this concern indicates that such overreliance can diminish students' decision-making and analytical reasoning abilities, as they may accept AI-generated outputs without sufficient scrutiny (Zhai et al., 2024). Additionally, educators are grappling with the ethical implications of AI use in classrooms. Research from the USC Center for Generative AI and Society (2024) highlights that teachers' ethical judgments about AI are influenced by factors such as gender and technological proficiency, affecting how AI is adopted and utilized in educational contexts.

To navigate these challenges, clear guidelines on AI usage are essential. The North Carolina Department of Public Instruction has developed a comprehensive chart delineating five levels of AI integration in assignments, ranging from no AI use to full AI use with human oversight. Each level specifies the extent of permissible AI involvement and outlines disclosure requirements, including citations and submission of AI interaction links. Implementing such structured frameworks can aid educators in setting transparent expectations, promoting ethical AI use, and fostering an environment where students can develop both technological proficiency and critical thinking skills.

	Level of AI Use	Full Description	Disclosure Requirements
0	*No AI Use*	This assignment is completed entirely without AI assistance. AI must not be used at any point during the assignment.	No AI disclosure required. May require an academic honesty pledge that AI was not used.
1	*AI-Assisted Idea Generation and Structuring*	No AI content is allowed in the final submission. AI can be used in the assignment for brainstorming, creating structures, and generating ideas for improving work.	AI disclosure statement must be included disclosing how AI was used. Link(s) to AI chat(s) must be submitted with final submission.
2	*AI-Assisted Editing*	No new content can be created using AI. AI can be used to make improvements to the clarity or quality of student-created work to improve the final output.	AI disclosure statement must be included disclosing how AI was used. Link(s) to AI chat(s) must be submitted with final submission.
3	*AI for Specified Task Completion*	AI is used to complete certain elements of the task, as specified by the teacher. This level requires critical engagement with AI generated content and evaluating its output. You are responsible for providing human oversight and evaluation of all AI generated content.	All AI created content must be cited using proper MLA or APA citation. Link(s) to AI chat(s) must be submitted with final submission.
4	*Full AI Use With Human Oversight*	You may use AI throughout your assignment to support your own work in any way you deem necessary. AI should be a 'co-pilot' to enhance human creativity. You are responsible for providing human oversight and evaluation of all AI generated content.	You must cite the use of AI using proper MLA or APA citation. Link(s) to AI chat(s) must be submitted with final submission.

Adapted by Vera Cubero for the North Carolina Department of Public Instruction (NCDPI) from the work of Dr. Leon Furze, Dr. Mike Perkins, Dr. Jasper Roe, & Dr. Jason Mcvaugh.

Common Classroom Applications

Elementary Examples

- **Teach students when they can use AI.** Sometimes, AI can be a helpful tool. Tell them, "You can use it when you're stuck thinking of ideas for a story or need help making your sentences sound better. It's okay to ask AI to help you understand a new word or check your spelling before you turn in your writing. You can even use it to quiz yourself before a test. Just remember, AI is there to help you think, not to do the thinking for you."

- **Teach students when they can't use AI.** But there are times when AI use is not appropriate. "You shouldn't ask it to do your whole assignment, like writing your book report or solving your math problems. That work is yours to try. It's also not okay to use AI during a quiz or test. I need to see your brain doing the work. And if AI helps you with something, don't pretend you did it all by yourself. Being honest about when and how you use AI is part of being a good learner and a good friend to your own learning."

Secondary Examples

- **Teach adolescents when they can use AI.** For secondary students, AI can be a powerful learning partner when used thoughtfully. "It's appropriate to use AI to help you brainstorm ideas for an essay, outline your thoughts, or improve the clarity of your writing. You might also use it to explore different ways to explain a concept you're struggling with, or to practice with sample questions before a test. In these cases, AI supports your thinking but doesn't replace it. You're still the one doing the learning. It just gives you a boost along the way."

- **Teach adolescents when they cannot use AI.** However, there are clear boundaries. "Using AI to write your entire assignment, solve problems without understanding them, or complete a test is not okay. That kind of use shortcuts the learning process and can create academic honesty issues. If AI generates content for you, you need to be transparent. Cite your sources, include a link to your chat, and be clear about what you used and why. Responsible AI use means knowing the difference between support and substitution. Your voice, your thinking, and your effort still matter most."

Strategy in Action

To introduce and use the AI Use Levels chart in the classroom, begin by explicitly teaching what each level means and why it matters for their learning. This can be done through a short lesson that connects the chart to broader conversations about academic integrity, responsible technology use, and the importance of human oversight when working with AI. Provide examples of your assignments that align with each level, making it clear when AI use is encouraged, restricted, or prohibited. It is also important to model how to disclose AI use properly, including how to link to AI chat transcripts and cite AI-generated content. Embedding the chart into assignment instructions, on classroom anchor charts, and within classroom routines can help normalize transparency and guide students to use AI tools in ways that support but do not supplant their learning. Over time, the chart becomes more than a policy document; it becomes a shared language for thinking critically about how AI fits into students' academic growth.

Teacher Moves

- Offer structured assignments with specific AI use levels (e.g., Level 2: You may use AI for editing only.).
- "Use AI to organize your ideas into an outline, but make sure you write the draft in your own words."
- Provide a model of what an AI disclosure statement looks like on a student assignment such as, "I used AI to brainstorm initial ideas and structure for the essay."

Student Moves

- Embed checkpoints in assignments where students must show handwritten notes, drafts, or reflections.
- Identify a performance level on a rubric for AI use transparency and critical reflection on its role (e.g., Level 3: Mentions AI use but lacks detail or critical reflection. Ethical considerations are vague or minimal.).
- Require a "thinking log" when AI is used—what it suggested, what was used, and what was rejected.

Extensions and Adaptations

- **Advanced learners:** Have students design a classroom policy or decision-making guide for AI use, with rationales based on research and ethical considerations, as well as district policy.
- **Multilingual learners:** Encourage students to explain how AI helped them bridge language gaps and reflect in writing or discussion on the differences between AI's wording and their own voice.
- **Emerging readers:** Create role-play activities where students act out scenarios of correct and incorrect AI use, discussing what good choices look like and why honesty matters.
- **Cross-content:** Have students track how their use of AI differs in math, ELA, or science, and reflect on how the purpose of the assignment shapes responsible AI use in each subject.

Skill Progression by Grade Band

Grade Band	Skills	Supports
K–2: Noticing Help Versus Doing the Work	• Recognize when they are thinking on their own • Identify when it's okay to get help (from a person or a tool) • Follow class rules about AI and tech use	• Visual prompts and icons for all my work/my work with some help/my work with a lot of help • Chart that shows different kinds of help • **Visual sort of appropriate vs. inappropriate technology use**
3–5: Exploring Safe and Fair Use	• Use AI for brainstorming or feedback with guidance • Explain how AI helped (or didn't) • Understand the difference between help and copying	• Reflection templates for "What AI Did/What I Did" • Scenarios about AI use for Think-Pair-Share discussions • **Set of classroom norms to follow when using any digital helper**
6–8: Making Purposeful Choices	• Decide when AI is helpful vs. harmful to learning • Reflect on how AI influenced their work • Begin citing or disclosing AI use when appropriate	• Reflection logs or exit tickets when working with AI • Simple AI output for student sorting and guided discussion • **Prompts for explanation and reflection of AI use**
9–12: Using AI With Judgment and Integrity	• Match AI use to task demands (e.g., idea generation vs. independent writing) • Evaluate the credibility of AI outputs • Cite and reflect on AI use transparently	• Access to citation and disclosure guidelines (e.g., APA/MLA for AI) • Protocol for deciding if and when to use AI • **Lesson plans on plagiarism and how to cite AI use**

online resources — Examples of the boldface supports above can be found on the book's companion website here: https://companion.corwin.com/courses/TeachingStudentsAI

Section 3

Teaching *With* AI

Learning Quests That Ignite Curiosity
and Deepen Understanding

OVERVIEW

We have suggested that AI shares some unexpected similarities with whales. In part, something massive is surfacing, but most of it lies beneath the surface. In this section, we focus not on what AI is, but how it can be used with purpose with your students. Just as marine biologists design their whale observations with care, teachers must design instructional experiences that help students interact with AI with intention and thought, and that improve learning outcomes. Our work on the gradual release of responsibility framework suggests that instruction needs to be responsive to students' learning needs and designed in ways that build students' competence and confidence (Fisher & Frey, 2021). We organize the intentional moves of teachers into four categories:

- Collaborative learning in which students work together to complete tasks
- Independent learning in which students practice and apply what they are learning
- Focused instruction, or the input from teachers
- Guided instruction and the systems of supports and scaffolds students need to be successful

Throughout this book, we have provided examples of teachers modeling and engaging in direct instruction. We have also noted the value of adaptive learning platforms in guiding students' thinking. We have also included several examples of students working with peers to solve problems and consolidate their understanding in the presence of peers. Thus, this section focuses mainly on creating tasks for students' independent learning that allow them the time and space to practice, apply or generalize, and receive feedback from AI systems. We've termed these experiences "quests."

A quest is more than a task. It's a structured learning experience in which students use AI to inform and support their thinking. Each quest highlights a specific way students can learn with AI: by comparing texts, analyzing claims, generating feedback, testing logic, or connecting new knowledge to prior ideas, to name a few. There are clear roles for teachers, students, and AI. In each quest, the teacher guides the purpose and structure, while AI helps personalize, extend, or clarify the learning process.

The quests support metacognition, strategy, inquiry, and growth. Teachers still plan, prompt, and scaffold. Students still do the thinking. But AI acts as a partner that, depending on the use, may amplify student voice, refine understanding, and deepen engagement.

You don't need to use, or teach, all 10 quests at once. Some teachers might launch a writing unit with a Growth Quest or close a science inquiry with a Reverse Quest. Others might combine a Mission Quest with an Anchor Quest to support interdisciplinary work. The quests have been designed to flex across content, grade level, and instructional style.

Each quest builds a different thinking habit, and each one aligns with the larger goal of preparing students to swim alongside AI, not just watch from the shore. The table below previews the 10 quests and highlights what makes each one distinct.

Quest	Core Purpose	What Makes It Unique
Anchor Quest	Connect new learning to core concepts or schema using AI to surface patterns.	Builds durable understanding through analogies and conceptual transfer.
Clarity Quest	Build self-awareness by using AI to resolve confusion and check understanding.	Emphasizes metacognitive checks. AI serves as a clarity coach.
Compare Quest	Analyze similarities and differences with AI to clarify key distinctions.	Strengthens contrastive reasoning. Focuses on insight, not judgment.
Critique Quest	Use criteria to evaluate quality with AI support for evidence-based feedback.	Focuses on judgment and improvement. AI helps refine, not just compare.
Growth Quest	Improve work through feedback and revision using AI as a thought partner.	Focuses on revision cycles. AI supports drafting and refining, not grading.
Level-Up Quest	Use AI-supported scaffolds that fade as students grow in independence.	Targets progression through complexity. AI scaffolds intentionally fade over time.
Mission Quest	Solve real-world, interdisciplinary problems using AI for research and design.	Applies learning to authentic challenges. Focuses on creation, not critique.
Perspective Quest	Explore topics through multiple viewpoints with AI as a dialogue partner.	Builds empathy and interpretive depth, not just contrast or debate.
Reverse Quest	Work backward from an outcome to explore logical or causal reasoning.	Supports backward thinking and reasoning reconstruction.
Right-Sizing Quest	Personalize access to content or tasks using AI to match readiness and interest.	Centers on choice and access. AI helps tailor input—not increase complexity.

 Examples of the boldface supports above can be found on the book's companion website here: https://companion.corwin.com/courses/TeachingStudentsAI

Anchor Quest

WHAT IS IT?

In an Anchor Quest, students use AI to connect new knowledge to a foundational idea, big concept, or personally meaningful context that serves as an anchor for learning. Rather than learning in isolated chunks, students build meaningful connections between what they already know and what they are learning. AI helps surface patterns, analogies, or overarching principles by acting as a cognitive bridge that strengthens understanding. This quest promotes deep learning with students developing durable, organized mental models that they can apply across subjects and out-of-classroom settings.

WHY IT MATTERS

Learning sticks when students can connect the new concept or skill to something meaningful and/or familiar. Whether it's a core concept, a lived experience, or a known framework, anchoring new knowledge helps students organize, retain, and *transfer* what they've learned. Without this, students may memorize content temporarily but struggle to use it flexibly. An Anchor Quest develops conceptual fluency, making learning both more coherent and more enduring.

HOW IT WORKS

Anchor Quest is grounded in research on schema activation, conceptual transfer, and analogical reasoning. When students connect new content to prior knowledge, they form mental frameworks (or schemas) that organize and give meaning to what they're learning. This process promotes retention and transfer across topics (Ambrose et al., 2010). Educational research consistently shows that helping learners identify and articulate patterns between concepts improves their ability to understand and apply those concepts flexibly. Analogical reasoning plays a key role in this work, especially when students are guided to compare unfamiliar ideas to more familiar ones in ways that highlight deep structural similarities (Richland & McDonough, 2010).

AI contributes to this process by serving as a reflective partner that prompts students to identify connections they might not immediately see. It can suggest meaningful analogies, ask guiding questions, or retrieve relevant prior knowledge based on student input. This supports metacognitive learning strategies like self-explanation, which are especially powerful when paired with AI-designed scaffolds (Holmes et al., 2019). In this way, Anchor Quest strengthens the cognitive pathways that make learning not only more durable, but more meaningful and transferable across classroom tasks and out-of-classroom contexts.

Common Classroom Applications

Elementary Examples

- **From seed to system.** Students connect plant life cycles to other natural systems.
  Prompt: "Help me find another system that works like a plant growing from a seed. What are some shared patterns?"
- **Math connections.** Students relate new math strategies to ones they've used before.
  Prompt: "I just learned to add with number lines. Help me link this to the way I used base ten blocks. What's similar?"
- **Anchoring words.** Students link new vocabulary to familiar words or experiences.
  Prompt: "The word is *migration*. Help me think of things I know that are like migration."

Secondary Examples

- **Theme threader.** In ELA, students connect the theme of a current text to earlier works or personally relevant issues.
  Prompt: "This novel is about freedom. Help me find another story or event from history or current life that explores freedom in a similar way."
- **Physics in the world.** Students anchor new physics concepts to everyday observations.
  Prompt: "I'm learning about friction. Help me find examples of friction happening in sports or daily activities."
- **From feudalism to firms.** In social studies, students link historical power systems to modern structures they recognize.
  Prompt: "Help me compare feudalism to how power works in a modern business. What's similar or different?"

Strategy in Action

To implement Anchor Quest effectively, model how to use core concepts as organizing frameworks. Begin with accessible examples and slowly increase complexity. AI can serve as a co-thinker, helping students identify connections they may not yet see. You can introduce anchor ideas to students by using AI tools that personalize learning and make abstract ideas increasingly concrete. For example, a chatbot can provide interactive explanations and real-time responses to student questions, helping them connect prior knowledge to new content.

Teacher Moves

- Introduce or review anchor ideas regularly.
- Prompt students to use AI to generate analogies or examples.

- Model how to trace a concept across multiple contexts.
- Highlight transfer moments between units or disciplines.
- Support students in building their own anchor maps or schema diagrams that show how new ideas connect to prior knowledge.

Student Moves

- Ask AI to help link new concepts to something familiar.
- Use AI to identify patterns across content areas.
- Reflect on why an anchor idea helps make sense of new material.
- Apply anchor concepts across subjects or out-of-classroom contexts.
- Create analogies or metaphors to describe new ideas.

Extensions and Adaptations

- **Advanced learners:** Have students create anchor maps tracing a core idea across multiple disciplines (e.g., *systems* in biology, civics, and economics).
- **Multilingual learners:** Use AI to translate and compare concept explanations across languages or cultures. Use AI to generate visuals and simple simulations tailored to different learning levels, ensuring all students grasp the core ideas.
- **Emerging readers:** Pair visuals with simplified AI summaries of anchor concepts.
- **Cross-content:** Use Anchor Quest in interdisciplinary projects (e.g., tying environmental science, policy, and civic engagement together with a core concept like *interdependence*).

Skill Progression by Grade Band

Grade Band	Skills	Supports
K–2: Early Connectors	<ul><li>Use pictures, stories, or familiar examples to connect new ideas</li><li>Ask AI to help find something they already know that is similar to a new concept</li><li>Begin to describe how a new word or topic reminds them of something else</li><li>Recognize patterns or familiar routines in learning tasks</li></ul>	<ul><li>Lessons on using AI tools to generate simple comparisons</li><li>Sentence stems for making connections ("It's like . . .")</li><li>**Chart with suggestions of ways to anchor your learning to familiar things**</li><li>Visual or story-based prompts that allow students to connect information</li></ul>

(Continued)

(Continued)

Grade Band	Skills	Supports
3–5: Concept Mappers	• Use AI to relate new ideas to previously learned content • Generate examples from personal experience or everyday life • Explain similarities between classroom content and real-world contexts • Identify recurring anchor ideas across lessons or subjects	• Checklists to identify steps for anchor concepts • **Graphic organizer to support higher level connections to topics of study** • AI prompts that link content to common experiences • Class anchor maps to model connections • Activity for sorting facts, ideas, sentences, and visuals to foundational ideas
6–8: Schema Builders	• Use AI to compare new and known concepts across subject areas • Build concept maps or diagrams showing thematic links • Use AI to generate analogies that connect prior and new knowledge • Explain how anchor concepts help them understand more deeply	• Graphic organizers for mapping learning and connecting ideas • AI-supported analogy tools and guiding prompts • Structured reflection prompts ("This reminds me of . . .") • Lessons on schema-building • **Anchor chart on different types of schema**
9–12: Cross-Disciplinary Synthesizers	• Use AI to generate cross-disciplinary connections through core concepts • Construct complex analogies to transfer understanding • Reflect on how anchor ideas shape their learning strategies • Apply anchoring to new subjects, tasks, or real-world challenges	• Cross-content concept mapping tools • Tools for reflection and schema transfer • **Tasks requiring interdisciplinary analogies or thinking** • Peer coaching or group synthesis tasks using shared anchor ideas

 Examples of the boldface supports above can be found on the book's companion website here: https://companion.corwin.com/courses/TeachingStudentsAI

Clarity Quest

WHAT IS IT?

Clarity Quest helps students utilize AI to better understand what they know, identify areas of uncertainty, and to move forward with additional confidence as a result. Rather than waiting for a teacher to point out confusion or misunderstanding, students can proactively engage AI to check their thinking, break down complex ideas, or clarify directions. This quest supports students in becoming more self-aware learners. In the Clarity Quest, AI functions as a metacognitive mirror by offering clarifications, modeling understanding checks, and rephrasing content so students can reflect and increase both self-awareness and clarity in real time.

WHY IT MATTERS

Learning is supported when students can recognize their own misunderstandings, spot gaps in their thinking, and take steps to resolve confusion. The Clarity Quest builds these abilities by encouraging students to engage in purposeful self-checks throughout the learning process. It helps learners become more independent, less reliant on external validation, and more comfortable navigating complexity. When students gain clarity, they gain control along with a stronger sense of agency and confidence. Also note: Clarity-seeking is a transferable ability across all learning, making it a generalizable metacognitive skill.

HOW IT WORKS

The Clarity Quest is grounded in research on metacognition and self-regulated learning. Specifically, it involves students' ability to monitor and direct their own understanding. Studies have emphasized the importance of metacognitive scaffolding, which are structured prompts or tools that guide learners to reflect, check understanding, and take control of their learning process (Azevedo & Hadwin, 2005). In Clarity Quest, scaffolds are designed to support understanding and clarity, rather than the more common scaffolds to support progression in task complexity. When students actively assess what they know and identify what's unclear, they are better able to plan, adjust, and retain new knowledge. This kind of self-monitoring is particularly valuable when it's embedded within instruction and the complete process of learning, rather than relegated to a final assessment (Panadero, 2017).

AI tools can support metacognitive development by offering just-in-time clarity prompts, adaptive feedback, and personalized explanations that students can request on demand. For example, as students use AI to restate directions, break down complex ideas, or ask follow-up questions, they're engaging in real-time self-regulation. AI-supported environments can improve learning outcomes when they support reflection and agency (Roll & Winne, 2015).

Common Classroom Applications

Elementary Examples

- **From confusion to clarity.** Students ask AI to explain instructions in simpler terms.

  Prompt: "I don't get what this question means. Can you explain it like you would to a third grader?"

- **Check my thinking.** Students summarize their understanding, then ask AI to spot what's missing.

  Prompt: "Here's what I think I just learned about the water cycle. Did I leave anything out?"

- **Vocabulary word pursuit.** Students use AI to clarify tough vocabulary in their own words.

  Prompt: "What does photosynthesis mean? Can you help me explain it in a way a kid could understand?"

Secondary Examples

- **Exploring and unpacking complex concepts.** Students ask AI to help unpack dense text or abstract ideas.

  Prompt: "I'm stuck on this sentence from the article. Can you explain it step by step, in simpler terms?"

- **AI as a quizzer.** Students write what they think they understand and ask AI to test them.

  Prompt: "I think I get the causes of the French Revolution. Ask me questions to make sure I understand."

- **Decoding difficult directions.** Students use AI to paraphrase complex task directions into manageable steps.

  Prompt: "This assignment has a lot of parts. Can you help me turn the directions into a checklist?"

Strategy in Action

Clarity Quest succeeds when students view their confusion as a signal to engage and seek understanding and clarity. Teachers can help normalize metacognitive help-seeking and guide students in using AI not for answers, but for insight. That early modeling helps students internalize what kinds of clarity they can, and should, seek through AI collaboration.

When a student recognizes that their understanding has been compromised or that they are not understanding the directions, they can use AI chatbots to engage in a dialogue about their learning. A student may prompt the chatbot by saying, "I'm confused about a section of the text I am reading. The author has introduced the following ideas (insert the ideas) and I need an explanation of these." This can set off a series of back-and-forth exchanges, building the student's understanding of the concepts such that they have better clarity and can return to the original learning text or task.

Teacher Moves

- Model how to ask AI for clarification, not just end-game answers or solutions.
- Encourage students to summarize their learning and then verify it with AI.
- Celebrate moments when students recognize and resolve confusion.
- Include regular "pause and clarify" routines in your instruction.
- Provide scaffolds to help students construct their own self-check prompts.

Student Moves

- Use AI to paraphrase instructions or feedback.
- Ask AI to explain concepts or test understanding.
- Reflect on which part of a task is unclear and why there is lack of clarity.
- Compare your own thinking with AI explanations to uncover alignment and gaps for pursuit of further understanding.
- Develop personalized strategies for getting unstuck that involve clarity-related AI use.

Extensions and Adaptations

- **Advanced learners:** Use AI to challenge students' understanding by introducing edge (extreme) cases or counterexamples.
- **Multilingual learners:** Ask AI to clarify or translate academic vocabulary in students' home languages and provide definitions and examples of the concepts.
- **Emerging readers:** Use voice-to-text features to ask AI for visual explanations or step-by-step summaries.
- **Cross-content:** Use Clarity Quest in any subject where instructions, vocabulary, or abstract concepts could become barriers. Students may ask for an analysis of the author's craft in an informational text to help understand the structure of the claims or arguments.

Skill Progression by Grade Band

Grade Band	Skills	Supports
K–2: Emerging Self-Checkers	• Use voice or drawing tools to explain confusion or ask for help • Ask AI to clarify instructions or vocabulary in simpler language • Recognize when something doesn't make sense and take action • Begin to name their thinking and identify misunderstandings	• Teaching prompts to model when and how to ask for help or clarity • **Chart with visuals for student use when seeking assistance** • Sentence stems for clarity ("Can you explain it more simply?") • Models and mentors that explicitly show what clarity means and why it is important
3–5: Developing Clarifiers	• Summarize what they understand before checking with AI • Use AI to clarify unfamiliar vocabulary or rephrase directions • Compare AI explanations with their own • Reflect on what part of a task was unclear and why	• Prompt starters for reflection ("I think it means . . . "/"Is that right?") • Side-by-side comparisons of personal vs. AI responses • Lesson on using AI to for clarity in a provided topic of study or prompt • **"Before you ask" clarity checklist**
6–8: Independent Interpreters	• Use AI to break down complex tasks or text • Identify gaps in understanding using AI-generated questions • Evaluate whether AI's explanation is complete or useful • Develop strategies for resolving confusion independently	• Graphic organizers for mapping confusion to clarification • **AI output analyzer focuses on clarity** • Models of strong vs. vague AI responses • Sentence frames for reflection ("AI helped me understand by . . . ")
9–12: Strategic Clarifiers and Evaluators	• Use AI to analyze and clarify abstract or multi-step tasks • Refine AI prompts to target specific gaps in understanding • Evaluate the reliability, bias, or helpfulness of AI explanations • Apply clarity-seeking strategies across subjects and assignments	• Prompt templates for breaking down complex directions with AI • Tracking system for confusion to clarification during research and other content area studies • **If . . . Then . . . scenarios for seeking assistance and clarification with/without AI** • Peer prompts for clarity-seeking techniques during partner and group work

 Examples of the boldface supports above can be found on the book's companion website here: https://companion.corwin.com/courses/TeachingStudentsAI

Compare Quest

WHAT IS IT?

A Compare Quest uses AI to help students examine two ideas, characters, time periods, texts, or theories side by side. Students collaborate with AI to explore similarities and differences, developing a deeper understanding of what makes each concept distinct or significant. Rather than stopping at surface-level traits, Compare Quests require students to analyze, interpret, and uncover meaningful insights through structured comparison. With AI's support, students test their thinking, clarify distinctions, and press beyond their initial observations. The process supports the development of academic reasoning and prepares students to communicate comparisons clearly and thoughtfully.

WHY IT MATTERS

Comparison is a cornerstone of critical thinking across disciplines, whether students are analyzing literature, evaluating historical events, or contrasting scientific theories. Engaging in structured comparisons helps learners develop conceptual clarity, deepen understanding, and build transferable reasoning skills. Recent research emphasizes the power of contrastive learning to enhance memory, generalization, and analytical depth (Siegler & Chen, 2008). At the same time, AI-supported learning environments have shown promise in helping students refine their comparisons with support from AI-powered feedback loops (Holmes et al., 2019). Compare Quests leverage these insights by giving students a structured, interactive space to notice, articulate, and reflect on meaningful distinctions.

HOW IT WORKS

Students begin by selecting or being assigned two items to compare—these might be characters, events, scientific models, texts, or social issues. They use AI to structure the comparison, ask clarifying questions, and reflect on the significance of what they discover. Instead of letting AI do the comparing, students evaluate AI-generated input and refine their own thinking. This aligns with principles of comparative reasoning (Gentner & Markman, 1997), which suggest structured comparison helps learners recognize meaningful patterns. Research on metacognition (Kuhn, 2005) and AI-supported learning (Holmes et al., 2019) further supports the role of prompting and feedback in helping students deepen understanding and retain concepts through active engagement.

Common Classroom Applications

Elementary Examples

- **Comparing characters.** Students use AI to explore how two characters in a story are alike and different.
  Prompt: "How are the main character and their friend similar and different?"

- **Switching seasons.** Students compare seasonal features using AI to build vocabulary and structure.
  Prompt: "What are some ways that summer and winter are the same and different?"

- **Exploring roles in the community.** Students explore jobs in the community and how they differ in purpose and tools.
  Prompt: "What are two ways these jobs are alike? How are they different?"

Secondary Examples

- **Historical movements comparison.** Students compare two significant historical events for causes and outcomes.
  Prompt: "How were the Civil Rights Movement and Women's Suffrage Movement similar and different in their strategies and impact?"

- **Literary theme analysis.** Students compare how two texts explore a shared theme.
  Prompt: "How do both authors show the idea of justice through their main characters?"

- **Scientific model review.** Students contrast scientific theories or models using AI to clarify technical differences.
  Prompt: "What are the key differences between the Bohr model and the quantum model of the atom?"

Strategy in Action

To implement Compare Quests, choose topics that are rich enough to allow for insight and allow students to press for deeper and more complex comparisons, not just obvious traits. Help students focus their thinking with guiding questions about purpose: Why compare these two things? What does the comparison reveal? AI can be used to model comparisons, provide feedback, or help students identify deeper contrasts and similarities. Facilitate the quest by supporting students in their efforts to organize, revise, and reflect on their findings in ways that emphasize clarity and meaning.

Teacher Moves

- Help students identify a strong comparison pair with potential for insight.
- Model how to prompt AI for structured comparison (e.g., Venn diagrams, contrast tables).
- Offer scaffolds for interpreting and evaluating AI responses.
- Encourage students to revise prompts to go deeper or clarify questions.
- Use checklists or criteria to support quality comparisons.

Student Moves

- Use a structured prompt to compare two ideas, texts, or concepts.
- Analyze AI feedback and refine or add new comparisons.
- Decide what distinctions are most meaningful or surprising.
- Organize findings using a structure (e.g., table, paragraph, diagram).
- Reflect on what the comparison helped them understand more deeply.

Extensions and Adaptations

- **Advanced learners:** Ask AI to compare two things from opposing theoretical lenses and critique the AI's framing.
- **Multilingual learners:** Provide an academic word bank that focuses on compare/contrast and similarities/differences terminology that students can use as they interact with AI systems.
- **Emerging readers:** Use AI-assisted Venn diagrams or comparison charts and voice-based input to describe differences.
- **Cross-content:** Use the Compare Quest format in math (e.g., linear vs. exponential growth), science (e.g., volcano types), or art (e.g., Impressionism vs. Cubism).

Skill Progression by Grade Band

Grade Band	Skills	Supports
K–2: Beginning Comparers	• Identify basic similarities and differences between familiar things • Use AI to describe or clarify how two items are alike or different • Express comparisons using words, drawings, or simple phrases	• Visual chart that shows different types of comparison • Graphic organizers designed for comparison (e.g., Venn diagrams) • Sentence stems for comparisons ("They are both . . . ," "One is . . . but the other is . . . ") • **Games for noticing, naming, and comparing**
3–5: Developing Distinction-Makers	• Use structured AI prompts to compare two concepts, characters, or events • Identify and categorize similarities and differences (e.g., appearance, role, impact) • Reflect on which comparisons are most meaningful	• Prompt starters for AI-supported comparisons and contrasts • Activity where students create comparison and contrast sorts for peers • Reflection frames for evaluating distinctions • **Chart of comparison-focused adjectives to help with nuanced and creative comparisons**
6–8: Analytical Comparers	• Analyze key similarities and differences with depth and nuance • Use AI to refine or extend their comparisons • Interpret the significance of contrasts and what they reveal	• Tools for layered comparison (e.g., multi-trait tables) • AI prompts for deeper synthesis and clarification • **Process chart for layered comparison and synthesis** • Peer protocols for engaging in comparison logic
9–12: Strategic Synthesizers	• Construct sophisticated comparisons across disciplines, texts, or time periods • Use AI to critique or challenge surface-level comparisons • Synthesize insights into clear arguments or original interpretations	• Matrix comparison organizers • AI critique and refinement prompts • Templates for comparative essays or debates with AI use • **Tracking tool for inquiry prompts and post-AI use reflection**

 Examples of the boldface supports above can be found on the book's companion website here: https://companion.corwin.com/courses/TeachingStudentsAI

Critique Quest

WHAT IS IT?

The Critique Quest has students using AI as a thought partner to evaluate the strengths and weaknesses of an idea, argument, model, or product. Moving beyond opinion, students apply clear criteria to assess quality, identify areas for improvement, and generate evidence-based critiques. AI assists by posing probing questions, surfacing gaps, or modeling evaluative reasoning. This quest strengthens students' analytical skills while cultivating respectful, constructive critique practices. The goal is not just to judge, but to think more deeply about what makes something *good*, *effective*, or *credible*, as well as why it meets or does not meet the criteria.

WHY IT MATTERS

Critique is an essential academic and career skill. Whether evaluating a peer's writing, an argument in a news article, or the design of a scientific model, students benefit from learning to assess quality with evidence and clarity. Engaging in critique helps students internalize what "good" looks like, deepens their understanding of content, and builds confidence in expressing informed judgments. It also fosters a classroom culture where improvement is seen as a shared goal, not a personal flaw.

HOW IT WORKS

Critique Quest is grounded in the principles of evaluative thinking and evidence analysis. Students learn to apply explicit criteria, such as clarity, evidence, logic, or effectiveness, while using AI to interrogate the quality of ideas or products. This process mirrors the cognitive moves described in critical thinking research (Facione, 2011), where reasoning, reflection, and self-regulation play key roles. Research also shows that structured critique, especially with guided support, improves both peer and self-assessment accuracy (Panadero, 2016). Unlike Compare Quests, which highlight similarities and differences, Critique Quests center on *quality*, in other words, how well something works, using explicit standards or rubrics.

AI supports this quest by prompting students to ask deeper questions, offering model critiques, or helping clarify evaluation rubrics. When students engage in critique with the aid of AI, they shift from vague opinion to purposeful analysis, strengthening their judgment and voice.

Common Classroom Applications

Elementary Examples

- **Book reviewers.** Students evaluate a book review using AI to identify vague claims and suggest stronger evidence.
  Prompt: "This review says, 'The book was interesting.' Explain why. What made it interesting? What evidence could be added?"

- **Design detectives.** Students critique a classmate's poster design using criteria for clarity, layout, and appeal.
  Prompt: "Here's my friend's poster. [Upload picture] Help me check: Is the title easy to see? Are the images helping the message?"

- **Claim checkers.** Students analyze simple opinion statements using AI to determine if the claim is supported.
  Prompt: "This sentence says chocolate milk is healthy. Help me check: What makes that true or not true?"

Secondary Examples

- **Argument analysis.** In a history essay, students critique the strength of evidence supporting a claim about a historical event.
  Prompt: "Review this paragraph. Is the evidence strong and specific? Help me suggest a better example if needed."

- **System model check.** In science, students assess a peer-created model of a system (e.g., the water cycle) using accuracy and completeness criteria.
  Prompt: "Use these science class criteria to critique this water cycle model. What works? What's missing?"

- **Pitch critique.** Students critique a peer's business idea or product pitch using AI to examine logic, feasibility, and persuasion.
  Prompt: "Here's the pitch. Use the rubric to check how logical and persuasive it is. Where could it be stronger?"

Strategy in Action

Critique Quest works best when students understand that critique is about growth, not judgment. Teachers should model respectful, evidence-based critique, then give students plenty of chances to practice with AI as a nonjudgmental partner. Early experiences can be guided and low stakes to build confidence.

Teachers can generate quality indicators with the class or provide them in advance. These quality indicators should be specific to the learning that students are doing and convey a range of performance or success. Students can then use these indicators such as, "the text includes robust academic language and powerful verbs," to analyze and critique a specific piece of work.

Teacher Moves

- Model a critique using a shared rubric or set of criteria.
- Emphasize respectful, constructive feedback.
- Prompt students to use AI to clarify vague feedback.
- Encourage students to explain their reasoning aloud or in writing.
- Guide students to revise their own work based on AI-supported critique.

Student Moves

- Ask AI to evaluate work using given criteria.
- Use AI to revise vague feedback into specific suggestions.
- Reflect on what makes something high-quality and why.
- Practice critiquing both peer work and anonymous examples.
- Use critique feedback (AI or peer) to revise and improve.

Extensions and Adaptations

- **Advanced learners:** Challenge students to critique complex arguments using multiple lenses (e.g., logic, ethics, effectiveness).
- **Multilingual learners:** Provide students with peer support and language partners to engage in peer review and critique collaboratively.
- **Emerging readers:** Provide visuals or audio prompts; use AI to simplify rubric language.
- **Cross-content:** Use in any subject where students produce work, such as critiquing solutions in math using mathematical reasoning, performances in music, or visuals in art.

Skill Progression by Grade Band

Grade Band	Skills	Supports
K–2: Foundational Feedback Givers	• Use simple language to say what they like or would change in a peer's work • Ask AI to help check if something makes sense or could be better • Recognize strengths or missing parts in a story or picture • Begin using criteria (e.g., "clear," "fun," "easy to follow") with support	• Model scenarios or role-play of most/least helpful critiques • Scaffolded feedback frames to be used for different purposes • **Critique quest anchor chart with common look-fors** • Feedback talk/response cards students can use to practice critiques
3–5: Emerging Evaluators	• Ask AI for help identifying what works well and what needs improvement • Use a checklist or simple rubric to guide critique • Explain feedback choices using simple reasoning ("I think it's better because . . . ") • Use AI to suggest specific improvements or questions to ask a peer	• Before and after texts for side-by-side comparison and discussion • Anonymous or shared writing samples for practice rounds • Critique questions and prompts to ask based on content area and topic • **"What would I prompt next?" activity where students practice asking AI for thoughtful critiques**
6–8: Thoughtful Critics	• Use AI to analyze clarity, logic, or effectiveness of arguments or designs • Critique work based on shared criteria and justify evaluations • Distinguish between helpful and vague feedback with examples • Revise critiques based on AI-supported reflection	• Prompt examples that can be used for prompt-refinement writing with this quest in mind • Criteria-based feedback evaluation tool • **Protocol for human–AI balanced writing (e.g., write, critique, revise, critique, edit)** • Sentence frames for critique justification ("This is stronger because . . . ")
9–12: Strategic Reviewers	• Use AI to evaluate strengths and weaknesses with precision • Analyze peer and AI feedback for relevance, bias, or quality • Apply critique across modalities (e.g., writing, presentations, designs) • Use critique as part of a broader improvement or peer review cycle	• Examples of AI-generated feedback and peer feedback for analysis and discussion • Tool for process tracking—comments, responses, and improvements • **"Say it better" activity where students analyze and critique the AI output to build deeper thinking with collaborative learning** • Integrated peer and AI feedback systems with reflection logs • Structured critique rounds with feedback and revision cycles

 Examples of the boldface supports above can be found on the book's companion website here: https://companion.corwin.com/courses/TeachingStudentsAI

Growth Quest

WHAT IS IT?

In a Growth Quest, students use the power of AI to analyze their work, gain additional perspectives, and support revision. A Growth Quest provides the opportunity to "revise and rise" through feedback and revision loops that lead to continuous, iterative improvement of their work.

WHY IT MATTERS

AI is a learning partner in a Growth Quest. Rather than a shortcut, AI offers a helpful voice that offers insight, while directly supporting reflection and revision. Students use AI to receive feedback and improve their work, while building stronger thinking habits in the process. Growth Quests help students receive more growth-supporting feedback that is both meaningful and personalized. AI can help teachers meet the demands of providing feedback that is just-in-time, just-for-them, given when and where it can do the most good (Brookhart, 2017). Great learning doesn't happen all at once but rather it grows through clear goals, support, and a willingness to revise.

HOW IT WORKS

Growth Quests are grounded in a cycle of purposeful feedback, reflection, and revision that is adaptable across disciplines and responsive to a diverse range of learner needs. As students interact with AI to receive feedback, they learn to evaluate suggestions, make strategic decisions, and refine their work over time. Along the way, they sharpen their skills in distinguishing help versus surface-level AI feedback. The goal isn't just to improve the product at the center of the quest; it's equally about growth in the process.

Research shows that high-quality feedback strengthens learning and supports transfer when it is timely, specific, and aligned to clear goals. Hattie and Timperley (2007) note that feedback that moves beyond corrective feedback is especially powerful. This includes feedback at the process level (the strategies used) and feedback at the self-regulation level (to promote reflection and self-monitoring). Interestingly, studies on adaptive technologies have further established that AI-powered feedback systems can increase student engagement and self-regulation when integrated thoughtfully into instruction (Xie et al., 2019).

Common Classroom Applications

Elementary Examples

- **Stretching stories with AI.** Students tell a story to an AI tool and use its feedback to extend the ending or add detail.

  Prompt: "Here's my story. Can you help me make the ending more exciting?"

- **Revising pictures using voice prompts.** Students describe a drawing to AI, then revise their explanation with more detail after hearing AI's response.

  Prompt: "This is my drawing. [Upload picture] What more could I say so someone understands it better?"

- **Strengthening abilities to support opinion.** Students write a short opinion paragraph and use AI to suggest ways to strengthen their reasons.

  Prompt: "Here's my opinion paragraph. Does my reason make sense, or should I add more examples?"

Secondary Examples

- **Enhancing arguments.** Students use AI to test whether their claim and evidence in a persuasive paragraph are clear and compelling.

  Prompt: "Is my claim strong, and does this evidence support it well? What can I improve?"

- **Tuning-up creative writing drafts.** Students revise a piece of descriptive or narrative writing based on AI's suggestions about tone or pacing.

  Prompt: "Does this part move too slowly or quickly? How could I make it better for the reader?"

- **Refining essays iteratively and intentionally.** Students use AI to critique and revise the structure and clarity of a multi-paragraph analytical essay.

  Prompt: "Review this essay for flow and clarity. Are the transitions and topic sentences strong?"

Strategy in Action

At its core, your role in a Growth Quest is to guide students through a revision process that strengthens thinking, not one that only improves the final product. Structure the experience around purposeful feedback, reflection, and intentional revision. You can use the steps across subjects and grade levels, but mindfully keep the focus on helping students make meaning through multiple revision cycles. Make sure to notice success when students begin to see revision as essential to learning, rather than just correcting errors.

Teacher Moves

- Introduce the Growth Quest task and clarify success criteria.
- Model how to write effective AI prompts aligned to the task.
- Guide students in interpreting AI feedback critically.
- Provide reflection prompts or sentence frames to support planning.
- Emphasize that revision is part of the learning, rather than simply fixing mistakes.

Student Moves

- Review the task and success criteria before drafting.
- Use structured prompts to request targeted feedback from AI, then revise prompts as necessary to generate relevant, actionable feedback.
- Critically evaluate AI suggestions and observations, and then decide what to apply and revise.
- Make thoughtful revisions that improve clarity or depth.
- Reflect on the multiple rounds of revision and the progression of changes.
- Reflect on and explain how their thinking and work improved through the revision process.

Extensions and Adaptations

- **Advanced learners:** Invite students to revise their AI prompts and complete additional feedback loops, comparing how the new feedback continued to shift their thinking.
- **Multilingual learners:** Encourage students to use their home language to reflect on changes and to access AI tools, pairing sentence frames in both English and their home language.
- **Emerging readers:** Offer visual revision journals where students draw their draft, feedback, and revision. Then, use AI voice tools to lower barriers while keeping the focus on reflection and revision to support and demonstrate learning.
- **Cross-content:** Have students apply Growth Quest strategies in additional subject areas. Then compare the revision experience across disciplines to help students further understand that revision is a transferable skill that supports thinking across disciplines.

Skill Progression by Grade Band

Grade Band	Skills	Supports
K–2: Early Revisers	• Use voice tools to tell a story or explain an idea • Listen to AI feedback and identify simple changes (e.g., "add a happy ending") • Respond to questions from AI with more detail • See revision as adding to or improving an idea	• Sentence stems for reflection on growth ("I changed . . . " or "Now I know . . . ") • Visual for a growth-focused learning process • Teacher-facing prompts for modeling positive change and growth • Timeline chart of class growth in a particular area • **Pictures and writing for growth analysis and guided discussion**
3–5: Intentional Improvers	• Use simple written or spoken prompts to ask for feedback • Identify one element of the work to improve (e.g., "make it clearer") • Choose which feedback to use (with teacher guidance) • Revise based on AI suggestions and explain the changes	• 3-column organizer to show growth (what I wrote, AI suggested, my revision) • **"Make this sentence better" activity using student-safe AI platforms for teacher-guided exploration** • Reflection sentence frames ("I made it better by . . . ") • Shared writing using collective intelligence (human-AI hybrid)
6–8: Reflective Refiners	• Write targeted prompts to improve clarity, structure, or logic • Interpret AI feedback independently and evaluate accuracy and usefulness • Apply selected suggestions and explain reasoning • Revise across multiple rounds and reflect on growth	• Protocol for peer debrief on AI feedback • Exit tickets for students to reflect on growth during one lesson, one week, one unit • Checklists to guide feedback evaluation and integration • **Sentence stems for metacognitive timeline-style reflection ("At first I thought . . . but now I see . . . ")**
9–12: Strategic Revisers	• Design specific, task-aligned prompts for feedback • Analyze AI feedback critically for precision, bias, or gaps • Synthesize multiple feedback sources (AI, peer, rubric) • Apply Growth Quest process across disciplines to support independent improvement	• Structured feedback and revision logs • Mentor prompts and feedback cycles for class discussion and learning • **"Pushback prompts" to stay in control of purpose, goal, and AI-generated supports** • List of different AI tools designed to support learning growth

 Examples of the boldface supports above can be found on the book's companion website here: https://companion.corwin.com/courses/TeachingStudentsAI

Level-Up Quest

WHAT IS IT?

A Level-Up Quest invites students to engage with increasingly complex learning experiences, supported by AI-generated scaffolds that fade over time. As students grow in skill and understanding, the supports they rely on gradually recede, helping them move from guided practice to confident independence. Teachers guide the process, but students are the ones doing the questing: setting goals, choosing challenges, and working with AI to navigate to the next level. This quest prioritizes access and progression, not shortcuts. It's a way to personalize the level of cognitive support on the path to greater independence while keeping expectations appropriately high, and to engage all learners in meaningful, challenging work.

WHY IT MATTERS

When students are supported just enough to succeed, and then challenged to stretch further, they grow in both competence and confidence. Level-Up Quests create entry points for all learners while keeping the bar high. This supports equity by offering responsive scaffolds that evolve with students, rather than fixed groupings or labels. With AI's help, scaffolds can be adapted in real time in ways such as clarifying language, rephrasing instructions, modeling thinking steps, or offering just-in-time hints (Hargrave et al., 2025). This quest engages students in challenging work and gives them the tools to rise to success (or level up) on their own terms.

HOW IT WORKS

The teacher introduces a task or topic that allows for multiple levels of complexity or depth. Students begin with AI-supported scaffolds, such as guiding questions, simplified texts, worked examples, sentence frames, or visual supports. Gradually fade those supports as understanding grows. Students use AI to request the help they need, and to shift the type or intensity of support as they level up.

This approach is grounded in zone of proximal development theory (Vygotsky, 1978), where growth happens in the space between what a student can do independently and what they can do with guidance. It also reflects principles of Universal Design for Learning (CAST, 2018), which emphasize flexible pathways and barrier reduction. Research confirms that scaffolding improves access and conceptual development, but warns that scaffolds are often underused and, when used, tend to be kept in place too long, sometimes indefinitely (Van de Pol et al., 2010). Level-Up Quests are designed to counteract that tendency by incorporating intentional fading that helps students transition from supported to independent performance. AI can assist in this fading process by letting students control the support level, re-prompt for help, or challenge themselves when ready.

Common Classroom Applications

Elementary Examples

- **Reading helper.** Students use AI to simplify a text before trying it independently.

  Prompt: "Can you explain this paragraph in simpler words? I'll try reading it by myself after."

- **Sentence building.** Students receive scaffolded support for writing sentences or short responses.

  Prompt: "Can you help me start my sentence about this book?"

- **Math model makeover.** Students study an AI-generated example of a math problem before solving their own.

  Prompt: "Show me an example of how to solve this kind of word problem."

Secondary Examples

- **Scaffolding arguments.** Students use AI to organize reasons and evidence before drafting an argument.

  Prompt: "Can you help me organize my ideas before I write my argument?"

- **Building science concepts.** Students use AI to explain a complex concept, then reduce support and check understanding.

  Prompt: "Explain mitosis step by step. Then quiz me to see if I understand."

- **Making source material accessible.** Students simplify a dense source with AI, then reread the original to apply their understanding.

  Prompt: "What's a simpler version of this article? Now help me go back and read the real thing."

Strategy in Action

To successfully implement a Level-Up Quest, begin with a rich task that can stretch in multiple directions. For example, deeper reasoning, greater independence, or broader connections. Help students identify their current level of confidence or skill, then use AI to provide just-right scaffolds. Over time, support students in reducing those scaffolds and reflecting on how their thinking has changed. The goal isn't speed, it's visible growth through thoughtful, supported progression.

Teacher Moves

- Design tasks that allow for varied levels of complexity and entry.
- Teach students how to use AI to request specific supports (not just answers).

- Monitor how and when students begin to fade supports and prompt reflection.
- Use formative assessment to adjust scaffolds as students progress.
- Encourage transfer of leveling-up habits to new subjects and challenges.

Student Moves

- Identify areas of struggle or uncertainty and request AI support.
- Use sentence frames, examples, or explanations to build understanding.
- Attempt more complex or independent versions of the task as skills grow.
- Reflect on what changed and how support helped them progress.
- Choose new challenges based on what they've mastered.

Extensions and Adaptations

- **Advanced learners:** Ask students to design their own scaffold-fade sequence or coach a peer through leveling up.
- **Multilingual learners:** Use AI to provide dual language supports or translate scaffolded content.
- **Emerging readers:** Use AI voice tools, diagrams, or audio explanations as alternate scaffolds.
- **Cross-content:** Apply Level-Up Quests to performance tasks (e.g., science investigations, art critiques, social studies simulations).

Skill Progression by Grade Band

Grade Band	Skills	Supports
K–2: Scaffold Starters	- Use AI to simplify instructions, explain unfamiliar words, or model simple tasks - Try a task with scaffolded help, then repeat it with less support - Notice when they no longer need a specific scaffold	- Visual to reflect on support (on my own, with a friend, with teacher help) - Gameboard style tracker of goals and progress - **Prompt cards and sentence stems for leveling up support** - Examples of using AI to get just-right help for teacher modeling

(Continued)

(Continued)

Grade Band	Skills	Supports
3–5: Scaffold Shifters	• Identify when and where support is needed • Use AI to get examples, hints, or clarifying explanations • Begin phasing out supports as confidence increases • Choose slightly harder tasks as skills grow	• **Goal and challenge sentence stems for beginning AI use** • Prompt progressions for scaffolded support • If . . . Then . . . scenarios for when to use AI as a leveling-up tool • Beginning list of student-safe AI tools and uses
6–8: Managing Complexity and Growth	• Choose appropriate AI tools to get help with structure, logic, or understanding • Challenge self by requesting reduced support or harder examples • Reflect on growth and adjust scaffolds accordingly • Transfer leveling-up strategies to new subjects	• Tool for reflecting on level of support needed and used • AI prompt guides aligned to specific unit goals • Tool to track student feelings while engaging with AI tools • **Chart for different levels of AI use—novice, growing, and ready to be on my own**
9–12: Self-Directed Progression and Transfer	• Design personal leveling-up sequences • Use AI strategically to tackle increasingly complex challenges • Mentor peers in identifying and fading scaffolds • Apply level-up strategies across subjects and tasks	• Ongoing list of available AI tools and uses • Text set for students to analyze for AI use (none, some, unsure) • **Chart mapping shortcuts vs. leveling up** • Protocol for using AI to level up work

 Examples of the boldface supports above can be found on the book's companion website here: https://companion.corwin.com/courses/TeachingStudentsAI

Mission Quest

WHAT IS IT?

A Mission Quest asks students to solve an authentic challenge by drawing on skills from multiple disciplines. These challenges might be rooted in science, civics, design, health, or the environment. Regardless, they require students to research, think critically, problem-solve, and communicate effectively. AI plays the role of an advisor, coach, or research assistant, helping students brainstorm, refine ideas, troubleshoot solutions, and prepare to present or publish their work. Mission Quests can be tackled as individual projects or collaborative team missions, with the goal of generating meaningful, creative solutions to complex problems.

WHY IT MATTERS

Mission Quests prepare students for the kinds of thinking they'll need beyond school, where challenges are messy, interdisciplinary, and typically unsolved. The process requires application of knowledge from multiple subjects to solve meaningful problems. As they engage in meaningful problem-solving, they grow in confidence, creativity, and awareness of the world around them. Mission Quest challenges can increase student engagement and promote purpose-driven learning. AI supports this process by offering guidance, options, and iterative feedback. Whether working individually or in teams, students gain agency and see how classroom skills transfer to real life.

HOW IT WORKS

Students begin by exploring a challenge, either teacher-designed or student-generated, that reflects a pressing issue. They then use AI to gather background knowledge, break the challenge into smaller components, and iterate on potential solutions. While students may consider multiple viewpoints, the focus of Mission Quest is on designing solutions, not analyzing perspectives for comparison or critique. For individual missions, students drive the process independently; in team missions, they may assume specific roles (e.g., researcher, designer, communicator) and use AI to support planning, collaboration, and communication. This mirrors principles of design thinking and project-based learning, where students cycle through problem-scoping, ideation, testing, and iteration.

When used intentionally, AI enhances this cycle by supporting just-in-time knowledge access, prompting reflection, and helping learners visualize or rehearse potential solutions (Holmes et al., 2019; Luckin et al., 2022). Studies on problem-based learning show that working on authentic, interdisciplinary challenges improves student motivation and strengthens conceptual understanding (Barron & Darling-Hammond, 2008). The key is not to let AI do the thinking; instead, AI helps students stretch, scaffold, and sharpen their ideas over time.

Common Classroom Applications

Elementary Examples

- **Lunchroom waste reduction.** Students work with AI to brainstorm ideas for reducing food waste in the cafeteria.

  Prompt: "Can you help me design a lunch system for my school that wastes less food, and also explain how it works?"

- **Inventors for a cause.** Students identify a problem in their community and invent a tool to solve it with AI's help.

  Prompt: "What is a problem kids in our town have? What could we invent to help solve it?" Remember that AI does not have access to current events, so remind them they need to consult other resources first before turning to AI.

- **Animal helpers.** Students design a machine or robot to help protect local wildlife.

  Prompt: "What kind of tool or robot could help protect animals from pollution?"

Secondary Examples

- **Messaging as community advocates.** Students use AI to craft persuasive messages for civic leaders about a local issue.

  Prompt: "What's a compelling way to frame this issue to persuade city leaders?" Remind them they need to consult other reliable sources, as AI cannot access current events.

- **Redesigning with STEM.** Students evaluate an existing product and work with AI to suggest improvements for sustainability or accessibility.

  Prompt: "What design changes could make this device more sustainable or accessible?"

- **Historical insights challenge.** Students use AI to draw lessons from the past that inform solutions to current issues.

  Prompt: "What lessons from past pandemics could inform a better response next time?"

Strategy in Action

To implement a Mission Quest, start with a challenge that is relevant, open-ended, and requires synthesis. Support students in identifying what knowledge and skills they'll need, then guide them in using AI as a thought partner. Encourage team members to collaborate on prompts and reflect on their roles using AI to clarify understanding or test different angles. For individual projects, emphasize ownership, iteration, and presentation of learning.

Teacher Moves

- Frame the mission with a driving question and authentic and reliable contextual information.
- Model how to break a complex challenge into smaller tasks using AI.
- Support research, design thinking, and problem-scoping with structured prompts.
- Help student teams clarify roles and coordinate efforts using AI tools.
- Scaffold reflection and revision throughout the mission cycle.

Student Moves

- Explore and define the mission challenge.
- Use AI to gather background knowledge, test ideas, and clarify concepts.
- Iterate on a solution using feedback, reflection, and teamwork (if applicable).
- Present or publish their work to an authentic audience.
- Reflect on both their product and process—what they learned and how they grew.

Extensions and Adaptations

- **Advanced learners:** Tackle more ambiguous or global challenges that require interdisciplinary sourcing and research-based expert feedback.
- **Multilingual learners:** Use AI to translate research or practice presentations in both English and their home language.
- **Emerging readers:** Use AI voice tools for brainstorming and planning, then use AI to storyboard the solution before moving to an ability-appropriate written narrative of the storyboard.
- **Cross-content:** Collaborate with another teacher to make the challenge span multiple subject areas (e.g., science + civics, ELA + health).

Skill Progression by Grade Band

Grade Band	Skills	Supports
K–2: Early Explorers	• Identify a simple real-world problem and describe it with support • Use AI to brainstorm possible solutions or gather ideas • Communicate a basic plan or invention with pictures and words	• Mission maps to track learning about a topic and different types of learning needed • Share experiences using AI to bring content area learning to life • **Mission role cards for student exploration** • Classroom "wonder wall" to use with teacher modeling of AI use
3–5: Budding Problem-Solvers	• Break a real-world challenge into manageable parts • Use AI to explore causes, solutions, and perspectives • Create and explain a solution that includes multiple steps or tools	• **Research checklists for learning about a new topic** • Prompt menus for AI-supported ideation ("What are three ways to solve this?") • Role cards for team-based challenges (e.g., researcher, designer, synthesizer) • Graphic organizers for mission planning and solution-building
6–8: Interdisciplinary Designers	• Tackle a complex problem requiring knowledge from multiple subjects • Use AI to iterate on solutions and test assumptions • Collaborate in teams to research, design, and present a solution	• Project management tools with built-in checkpoints • **Role-based AI prompts for collaborative problem solving** • Examples of real-world interdisciplinary solutions for analysis
9–12: Strategic Innovators	• Define and refine a real-world challenge independently or collaboratively • Use AI as a partner to brainstorm, research, revise, and present a solution • Present or publish work for authentic audiences and reflect on impact	• Student-created mission planning templates that include role, purpose for role, and AI prompts to use • Protocol for using tools to rehearse and refine presentations (e.g., speech practice, infographic creation, slide deck support) • Organizers to gather evidence from different disciplines • **List of AI tools that help with presentation and delivery of content**

 Examples of the boldface supports above can be found on the book's companion website here: https://companion.corwin.com/courses/TeachingStudentsAI

Perspective Quest

WHAT IS IT?

A Perspective Quest engages students in exploring a topic, character, issue, or event from multiple viewpoints or cultural lenses. In this quest, AI serves as a dialogue partner that encourages students to test assumptions, encounter unfamiliar perspectives, and expand their thinking. It supports empathy, critical analysis, and narrative complexity not by offering answers, but by helping students ask deeper, more nuanced questions. The quest is designed to help students go beyond surface-level understanding and engage with complex, sometimes conflicting, interpretations.

WHY IT MATTERS

Perspective-taking is a foundational skill for civic life, academic discourse, and personal growth. When students actively engage with diverse perspectives, they can develop empathy, critical thinking, and the ability to navigate complex social issues. AI tools can scaffold this process by offering voices and lenses students may not otherwise encounter. As a result, Perspective Quests foster meaningful dialogue and cultural awareness, while helping educators emphasize diverse viewpoints and helping students experience the value of diverse perspectives firsthand.

HOW IT WORKS

Unlike a Compare Quest, which examines ideas or features side by side, Perspective Quests emphasize how identity, experience, and context shape understanding, especially when perspectives may conflict or defy categorization. Students begin with a central topic or prompt—this might be a character decision, historical event, or social issue. They then use AI to simulate or surface alternate viewpoints, engaging in structured cycles of reflection, comparison, and analysis. The goal is not to adopt all viewpoints but to understand how context, experience, and culture shape interpretation. This approach aligns with dialogic pedagogy (Wegerif, 2013), supports development of metacognitive skills (Zohar & David, 2009), and encourages intercultural understanding (Banks, 2005). AI becomes a catalyst for productive struggle, encouraging students to grapple with complexity and resist binary thinking.

Common Classroom Applications

Elementary Examples

- **Character point of view.** Students explore how a different character might feel about a shared event.

  Prompt: "How might the little sister in the story feel about the main character running away?"

- **Multiple voices on school rules.** Students consider how different people would view a change at school.

  Prompt: "How might a parent, a teacher, and a student each feel about the new lunch rule?"

- **Global folktale analysis.** Students compare folktales from different cultures using AI to uncover variations.

  Prompt: "What is a story from another culture where an animal plays a trick?"

Secondary Examples

- **Historical perspective shifter.** Students explore a past event through the eyes of multiple stakeholders.

  Prompt: "Describe the Boston Tea Party from the perspective of a British official, a colonist, and a Loyalist merchant."

- **Debate rehearsal.** Students engage in argument practice with AI providing counterpoints.

  Prompt: "What are some thoughtful counterarguments to the claim that social media should be banned in schools?"

- **Character lens awareness.** Students use AI to examine a theme through different characters' viewpoints.

  Prompt: "How would Atticus and Scout each describe what courage means after the trial?"

Strategy in Action

To implement Perspective Quests intentionally, begin with a rich, open-ended question or task. Clarify for students why exploring multiple viewpoints matters, and how AI can be used as a tool for broadening understanding, not just fact-finding or single-answer pursuits. Provide scaffolds that help students think critically about each perspective, and create structured spaces for them to reflect, revise, and synthesize what they've learned.

Teacher Moves

- Frame the quest around a rich, debatable topic or theme.
- Model how to prompt AI for alternate or underrepresented perspectives.
- Teach students to evaluate AI responses for authenticity, bias, or surface-level generalizations.
- Provide sentence stems to support comparative analysis or reflective writing.
- Create space for discussion, disagreement, and discovery.

Student Moves

- Identify the central idea, event, or decision they're examining.
- Use structured AI prompts to surface different perspectives.
- Evaluate the tone, assumptions, and completeness of each perspective.
- Compare insights and reflect on how their thinking changed.
- Synthesize what they learned into writing, dialogue, or creative expression.

Extensions and Adaptations

- **Advanced learners:** Create AI prompts that intentionally provoke bias or simplification, then critique the response and revise it for nuance.
- **Multilingual learners:** Use AI to explore how cultural values influence a topic in different parts of the world, using bilingual prompts.
- **Emerging readers:** Use voice tools to ask perspective questions and draw what each character or person might say or do.
- **Cross-content:** Pursue Perspective Quests in other disciplines such as science (e.g., animal conservation), social studies (e.g., border policy), or health (e.g., nutrition advertising).

Skill Progression by Grade Band

Grade Band	Skills	Supports
K–2: Early Empathy Builders	<ul><li>Describe how a familiar character or person might feel in a situation</li><li>Use AI to ask what someone else might think or say</li><li>Compare simple viewpoints using pictures or spoken ideas</li></ul>	<ul><li>**List of student-safe AI tools that simulate responses**</li><li>Sentence starters for feelings and viewpoints ("She might feel ___ because ___.")</li><li>Collection of prompts and images for a sort or guided discussion</li><li>Teacher modeling of using AI to explore varying perspectives</li></ul>
3–5: Perspective Explorers	<ul><li>Ask AI to explain how different people might view a situation</li><li>Identify and compare multiple viewpoints on a topic or event</li><li>Reflect on how hearing new perspectives changes their own thinking</li></ul>	<ul><li>Prompt menus for viewpoint comparison</li><li>"Walk in their shoes" activity using AI to explore different perspectives</li><li>**Organizer for looking at one topic through different lenses**</li><li>Role-play scenarios for students to practice how they would respond</li></ul>
6–8: Analytical Perspective Takers	<ul><li>Examine how background, culture, or experience shapes viewpoint</li><li>Use AI to simulate alternate lenses and challenge assumptions</li><li>Evaluate tone and bias in different perspectives</li></ul>	<ul><li>Organizer to guide exploration of stakeholders and accompanying perspectives on a topic</li><li>Bias checklists and evaluation rubrics</li><li>**AI-generated images to use for guided discussion on any present bias**</li><li>Sentence stems for comparing and critiquing viewpoints</li></ul>
9–12: Nuanced and Critical Interpreters	<ul><li>Prompt AI for underrepresented or global perspectives on complex issues</li><li>Critique and refine AI responses for depth, bias, and nuance</li><li>Synthesize multiple perspectives in arguments, creative works, or debates</li></ul>	<ul><li>Comparative analysis templates for written or oral synthesis</li><li>Models of diverse and authentic perspectives for reference</li><li>Tools for annotating or coding AI-generated perspectives</li><li>**Collection of articles and texts about the dangers of bias in AI**</li></ul>

 Examples of the boldface supports above can be found on the book's companion website here: https://companion.corwin.com/courses/TeachingStudentsAI

Reverse Quest

WHAT IS IT?

A Reverse Quest challenges students to work backward from an answer, outcome, or conclusion to determine how it might have originally been reached. Students must reconstruct reasoning, test possibilities, and explain the process that could have led to a given result. This promotes deeper thinking by shifting focus away from "getting the right answer" to exploring multiple scenarios and pressing for understanding about how thinking works. In a Reverse Quest, AI serves as a dynamic assistant by supporting the posing of questions, testing of logic, and exploration of alternate pathways that each could lead to the same result. Relevant to any content, from STEM to humanities, Reverse Quests foster curiosity and strategic thinking, while deepening understanding of cause and effect.

WHY IT MATTERS

Reverse Quests help students practice logical reasoning, strategic inquiry, and evidence-based explanation. By starting with a result and working backward, they press for a deeper understanding of structure, process, and causality. As they engage, their analytical thinking is strengthened. AI enhances this process by modeling reverse reasoning, testing logic, and prompting students to explore alternate paths. Comprehension and flexible thinking are key and essential skills for navigating uncertainty and complexity in school and life. Unlike Perspective or Mission Quests, Reverse Quests don't focus on adopting viewpoints or proposing forward solutions. Instead, they sharpen students' ability to deconstruct and reconstruct reasoning based on a known outcome.

HOW IT WORKS

The teacher provides an outcome, such as a final number, a historical result, a resolved conflict, or a completed project. Students must determine what steps, choices, or conditions could have led to it. Students use AI to explore, refine, and test reverse pathways, treating AI as both a partner in speculation and a critic of plausibility. In math, this might mean figuring out what equation results in a known answer. In English Language Arts, it might mean constructing a backstory for a character's final decision.

This approach is grounded in backward problem-solving and reverse engineering principles, which research shows can improve understanding of both content and structure (Jonassen, 2011; Zhong et al., 2024). When students reason backward, they engage metacognitive strategies that strengthen transfer and error analysis. AI tools that support reverse thinking by modeling alternate routes or surfacing hidden steps amplify this process and help students learn to think both forward and backward.

Common Classroom Applications

Elementary Examples

- **Mystery with math.** Students work backward from a solution to identify possible equations or number combinations.

  Prompt: "The answer is 24. What are two different ways I could have gotten that using division?"

- **Story ending pursuit.** Students invent backstories to explain how a surprising or unusual ending came to be.

  Prompt: "A story ends with 'and the bear gave her the map.' What could have happened to make that the ending?"

- **Figuring science failures.** Students examine a failed science result and hypothesize possible errors.

  Prompt: "If the plant died in the experiment, what could have gone wrong with how we set it up?"

Secondary Examples

- **Rebuilding algebra equations.** Students use a known solution to work backward and generate plausible equations.

  Prompt: "If the answer is $x = 3$, what equation could have that as the solution, and how do you know?"

- **History rewound.** Students reconstruct the key events that led to a significant historical turning point.

  Prompt: "What could have led to the fall of the Berlin Wall? Explain the key moments that made it possible."

- **Literary backtracking.** Students develop a psychological or situational explanation for a character's final decision.

  Prompt: "Why did the main character decide to forgive their friend? What might have changed their mind?"

Strategy in Action

To implement a Reverse Quest effectively, choose an end point that invites multiple valid pathways, not just one correct answer. Use prompts and AI tools to help students explore possible reasoning, simulate outcomes, and compare interpretations. Emphasize that this is not guesswork. Instead, it's strategic reconstruction that rewards curiosity and logic. Whether working individually or in groups, students should reflect on the plausibility and clarity of their backward thinking.

Teacher Moves

- Choose compelling outcomes that invite reconstruction and interpretation.
- Model how to work backward using AI as a logic or plausibility checker.
- Provide prompts that help students test, simulate, or explain backward paths.
- Support iteration and comparison of multiple possible routes.
- Use graphic organizers to help map out reverse thinking (e.g., reasoning trees).

Student Moves

- Analyze the given outcome and brainstorm what might have led to it.
- Use AI to test different backward paths and evaluate which make the most sense.
- Explain their reasoning clearly, with evidence or logical steps.
- Revise their thinking based on new information or feedback.
- Reflect on what they learned about the process, not just the answer.

Extensions and Adaptations

- **Advanced learners:** Ask AI to generate multiple backward paths and critique the quality or logic of each.
- **Multilingual learners:** Use bilingual AI prompts to explore reasoning in both English and their home language.
- **Emerging readers:** Use AI voice tools to narrate or draw reverse paths step-by-step.
- **Cross-content:** Use Reverse Quests in P.E. (e.g., how did we lose that game?), music (how was this song built?), or health (how could this symptom have developed?).

Skill Progression by Grade Band

Grade Band	Skills	Supports
K–2: Beginning Reverse Thinkers	• Explore simple outcomes and brainstorm what could have caused them • Use AI to generate ideas for how something might have happened • Describe steps or events that could lead to a known ending	• Written or visual cards for backward story mapping • "How did it happen?" picture cards with prompts (e.g., "What happened before?" or "How did they get here?") • **Shared writing using AI to backward plan a story**
3–5: Early Reasoners and Reconstructors	• Identify multiple ways a result could occur • Use AI to test different backward paths • Explain which path makes the most sense and why	• **Backward reasoning sort and reflection** • Prompt starters ("What could have happened before . . . ?") • AI-powered examples of different reverse solutions • Checklists to compare logic and discuss outcomes
6–8: Strategic Reverse Analysts	• Reconstruct reasoning or decision-making processes from known outcomes • Use AI to test assumptions, simulate outcomes, and refine logic • Reflect on alternative paths and compare plausibility	• AI simulations or scenario builders • Sentence frames for reverse explanations ("If ___ then ___, because ___.") • **Peer review protocols for checking logical reasoning** • Historical or narrative case study sets for practice
9–12: Critical Reverse Engineers	• Design and critique multiple reverse paths to a given result • Use AI to examine causal logic, test hypotheses, and refine explanations • Apply reverse thinking to argument, analysis, or systems across subjects	• **Tools for generating and mapping alternate reasoning paths** • AI prompts for modeling, testing, and critiquing logical flow • Guided templates for historical, literary, or scientific backward analysis • Example of using AI to deconstruct a claim (What could lead to this claim?)

Examples of the boldface supports above can be found on the book's companion website here: https://companion.corwin.com/courses/TeachingStudentsAI

Right-Sizing Quest

WHAT IS IT?

In a Right-Sizing Quest, students use AI to customize how they access, engage with, and demonstrate learning—choosing formats, supports, or starting points that meet them where they are. Rather than assigning one-size-fits-all content or tasks, teachers guide students to use AI tools that adjust format, language, or level of support to match their current readiness or interests. The goal is not to lower expectations, but to increase access and agency. Focused on choice and fit, AI acts as a flexible *differentiator*, helping students tailor their experience based on readiness, interest, or need, while staying aligned to core learning goals.

WHY IT MATTERS

Differentiation is essential for equitable learning, but it's also challenging to do well. Right-sizing empowers students to take an active role in shaping and individualizing their learning experience, which fosters both autonomy and engagement. When learners are given options and tools to find the version of a task or text that works best for them, they are more likely to persist, participate, and succeed. This quest helps ensure that students not only receive content, but also connect with it.

HOW IT WORKS

Right-sizing is grounded in the principles of Universal Design for Learning, which emphasize providing multiple means of engagement, representation, and expression to support learner variability (CAST, 2018). Differentiation through dimensions of choice and access allows students to engage with content at a pace, format, or complexity level that fits their current readiness. It allows this to be accomplished without compromising rigor. When students can select how they access and express understanding, they are more motivated and develop a stronger conceptual grasp (Hall et al., 2015).

Recent studies on personalized learning environments highlight the power of adaptive technologies to support equitable access. For example, AI-powered tools can dynamically adjust content presentation by simplifying language, suggesting alternate formats, or offering conceptual prompts based on learner input (Chen et al., 2020). In a Right-Sizing Quest, this means students might use AI to rephrase instructions, request an alternate example, or select from differentiated tasks. Any of these interactions stands to provide more control over how they engage while staying focused on shared learning goals.

Common Classroom Applications

Elementary Examples

- **Choose your challenge.** Students select from three AI-assisted versions of a math word problem.

    Prompt: "Show me this math problem with easier numbers but the same steps."

- **Multiple ways to read.** Students explore a nonfiction text with options for simplified summaries, key facts, or audio narration.

    Prompt: "Can you give me a version of this article that's shorter and easier to understand?"

- **Pick your prompt.** Students choose writing prompts at different readiness levels but aimed at the same skill.

    Prompt: "I'm ready to write about animals. Can you give me a fun, easy question to start with?"

Secondary Examples

- **Text tailoring.** Students use AI to simplify or annotate a complex article before reading.

    Prompt: "Can you rewrite this paragraph at a ninth-grade reading level and explain the hard parts?"

- **Same goal, multiple paths.** Students are offered choice-based opportunities to demonstrate their learning, for example a choice between responding to a podcast, article, or image set on the same historical topic.

    Prompt: "Give me three ways I could learn about the Civil Rights Movement—pick one that uses visuals."

- **Writing task selector.** Students use AI to find a version of a writing task that suits their confidence level.

    Prompt: "I want to start with an easier version of this writing task, but still meet the goal. Can you help?"

Strategy in Action

The Right-Sizing Quest works best when teachers frame choice as a path to equity. Students should understand that selecting the right level of challenge isn't about doing less. Rather, it's about doing what works to reach success. Teachers guide students in selecting tools and pathways that support growth while reinforcing shared expectations for learning outcomes.

Teacher Moves

- Offer clear learning targets, then invite student choice in approach.
- Provide AI tools or prompts that adjust text, format, or level.
- Normalize different entry points without labeling students.
- Model how to use AI to tailor a task while keeping the rigor.
- Monitor choices and provide coaching to support self-awareness.

Student Moves

- Use AI to simplify content or translate vocabulary.
- Choose from different formats or starting tasks.
- Reflect on what kind of support helps them most.
- Ask AI to reframe or restate tasks for better clarity.
- Pursue shared learning goals through formats and entry points that best support individual growth.

Extensions and Adaptations

- **Advanced learners:** Use AI to add layers of complexity or connect to more abstract ideas.
- **Multilingual learners:** Translate prompts, adjust reading levels, or generate bilingual supports.
- **Emerging readers:** Ask AI for visual explanations, audio supports, or sentence starters.
- **Cross-content:** Use in any subject where learners can meet goals through varied resources or modalities.

Skill Progression by Grade Band

Grade Band	Skills	Supports
K–2: Access Explorers	<ul><li>Ask AI to read aloud or simplify short instructions</li><li>Use voice or picture prompts to choose learning options</li><li>Recognize when a task feels too hard or too easy</li><li>Make simple choices about how to show understanding (e.g., draw, tell, act)</li></ul>	<ul><li>"Pick Your Path" scenario cards for practice and discussion</li><li>Simplified choice boards or menus with AI integration</li><li>Sentence frames for expressing needs ("I want to try . . . because . . ." or "I want to do . . . so I think I should try . . .")</li><li>**"A Lot of Help" vs. "A Little Help" scenario cards for sorting and discussion**</li></ul>
3–5: Flexible Learners	<ul><li>Use AI to rephrase text or break a task into steps</li><li>Choose from multiple formats to access or express learning</li><li>Reflect on which version of a task or explanation works best</li><li>Use AI to explore topics or examples that match personal interests</li></ul>	<ul><li>Prompt banks for adjusting complexity or focus of texts</li><li>**"Getting help the right smart way" classroom chart and prompts**</li><li>Tiered task menus and ways AI can support at each level (getting started, ready to go, challenge me)</li><li>Use of familiar content to support differentiated access</li></ul>
6–8: Personalized Navigators	<ul><li>Use AI to adjust the complexity or length of content</li><li>Select from differentiated tasks aligned to the same objective</li><li>Explain why a certain format or approach supports their learning</li><li>Use AI to tailor vocabulary or scaffolding supports</li></ul>	<ul><li>**Guided comparison and ranking of original vs. AI-supported content**</li><li>Learning logs or quantitative reflection systems to track what worked best</li><li>Lessons on using AI to tailor content without changing integrity of the texts</li><li>Activities where students are assigned the same learning goal but have options for presentation and product</li></ul>
9–12: Independent Differentiators	<ul><li>Make strategic choices about task versions or entry points</li><li>Use AI to right-size content based on learning goals and self-awareness</li><li>Evaluate how different supports impact comprehension or performance</li><li>Transfer right-sizing strategies across disciplines and formats</li></ul>	<ul><li>Tool for documenting and justifying task choices</li><li>Prompts for creating and building self-selected scaffolds based on learning needs and assignment goals</li><li>**Prompt cards to assign students different ways to use AI to change a task with the same learning goal in mind**</li></ul>

 Examples of the boldface supports above can be found on the book's companion website here: https://companion.corwin.com/courses/TeachingStudentsAI

CONCLUSION

Let's return to where we began, the boat.

At first, there was fog. Silence. A few hopeful glances toward the horizon. You might remember the splash we imagined and the moment that confirmed what many of us had only sensed before: A powerful force was rising just beneath the surface of our work. We're talking, of course, about artificial intelligence.

In the pages that followed, we've moved closer to that "something," not to control it, but to understand it. And more importantly, to help our students understand it. We considered how to teach *about* AI so students can see what it is, how it works, and how it fits into the broader world. We explored teaching *with* AI by introducing classroom quests that help students interact with AI in meaningful, scaffolded, and creative ways. And we pulled back the curtain to teach *for* AI by strengthening the human intelligence skills that matter most. These included curiosity, critical thinking, ethical reasoning, and metacognition.

Together, these three perspectives—teaching *about*, *with*, and *for* AI—offer a human-centered vision of what it means to integrate artificial intelligence into K–12 classrooms. These efforts are not about using technology for its own sake. They're about helping students think and thrive in a world where AI becomes a natural, ever-present part of the ecosystem.

So where does that leave us now? Right here: Watching the water. With a bit more confidence and a much clearer sense that this isn't something to fear. It's something to teach.

A FEW PRINCIPLES TO KEEP US ORIENTED

As we continue learning and leading in a time of rapid change, it helps to have some grounding principles. The points that follow come from Ethan Mollick's *Co-Intelligence* (2024), and they offer four practical truths for working with AI that we have applied to the classroom setting.

1. **Always invite AI to the table.** Like any tool, AI becomes more valuable when paired with purpose and intent. You might prompt it to summarize student writing for feedback discussions, brainstorm lesson starters, or generate examples tailored

to specific learning needs. Students can use it to explore ideas before writing, check their understanding, or generate questions they hadn't thought to ask. The more thoughtfully we incorporate AI, the more we help students see it as a resource they can learn to use well.

2. **Be the human in the loop.** AI doesn't know your students. It doesn't know your goals. It doesn't know the culture and relationships in your classroom. Only you do, which is why your role remains essential. Use your judgment to refine prompts, question AI's suggestions, and model how to check its responses. When students use AI, teach them to pause and ask: Does this make sense? Is it accurate? Is it ethical? The pause and that human moment are key to successful use of AI in the classroom.

3. **Treat AI like a person, tell it the kind of person to be, and remember that it's not human.** AI can sound very fluent, even human-like. It can role-play, it can explain, it can even debate. But AI doesn't understand context or consequences. While students might treat it like a conversation partner, they also need to remember it's not a peer, a teacher, or a source of truth. We can encourage playful and productive use, while still helping students verify, question, and critically evaluate what AI offers.

4. **Assume this is the worst AI you'll ever use.** Today's tools are powerful, but they're just the beginning. Tomorrow's systems will be faster, more accurate, and more deeply integrated into daily life. That's why this book has focused on skills, knowledge, and mindsets that will uphold as AI evolves, rather than specific AI tools that will continue to evolve and expand. By teaching students to think alongside AI, we prepare them to meet a future we can't fully predict with curiosity, clarity, and care.

A FINAL THOUGHT

You don't have to be an expert in AI to help your students explore it. But you must be willing to start the conversation. To let them ask questions. To let yourself wonder. To try a prompt and see what happens. Bring your binoculars. Watch the surface. Stay curious. And when the whale inevitably breaches again, you'll be ready to say, "I see it! Let's follow."

REFERENCES

Ambrose, S. A., Bridges, M. W., DiPietro, M., Lovett, M. C., & Norman, M. K. (2010). *How learning works: Seven research-based principles for smart teaching*. Jossey-Bass.

American Association of School Librarians. (2018). *National school library standards for learners, school librarians, and school libraries*. ALA.

American Association of School Librarians. (2025). *National school library standards* (2nd ed.). Author.

Anthonysamy, L. (2021). The use of digital technologies for formative assessment: A systematic review. *Computers & Education*, 168, 104212.

Azevedo, R., & Hadwin, A. F. (2005). Scaffolding self-regulated learning and metacognition: Implications for the design of computer-based scaffolds. *Instructional Science, 33*(4), 367–379. https://doi.org/10.1007/s11251-005-1272-9

Banks, J. A. (2005). *Cultural diversity and education: Foundations, curriculum, and teaching* (5th ed.). Pearson Education.

Barron, B., & Darling-Hammond, L. (2008). Teaching for meaningful learning: A review of research on inquiry-based and cooperative learning. In L. Darling-Hammond, B. Barron, P. D. Pearson, A. H. Schoenfeld, E. K. Stage, T. D. Zimmerman, G. N. Cervetti, J. L. Tilson, & M. Chen (Eds.), *Powerful learning: What we know about teaching for understanding* (pp. 11–70). Jossey-Bass.

Bedley, S. (2017, March 29). I taught my 5th graders to spot fake news. Now they won't stop fact-checking me. *Vox*. https://www.vox.com/first-person/2017/3/29/15042692/fake-news-education-election

Bereiter, C., & Scardamalia, M. (2014). Knowledge building and knowledge creation: One concept, two hills to climb. In S. C. Tan, H. J. So, & J. Yeo (Eds.), *Knowledge creation in education* (pp. 35–52). Springer.

Bloom, B. S. (1984). The 2-sigma problem: The search for methods of group instruction as effective as one-to-one tutoring. *Educational Researcher, 13*, 4–16.

Brainard, L. (2025). The curious case of uncurious creation. *Inquiry, 68*(4), 1133–1163.

Brookhart, S. M. (2017). *How to give effective feedback to your students* (2nd ed.). ASCD.

Burtell, M., & Toner, H. (2024, March 8). *The surprising power of next-word prediction: Large language models explained, Part 1*. Center for Security and Emerging Technology.

CAST. (2018). *Universal Design for Learning guidelines version 2.2*. http://udlguidelines.cast.org

Center for Security and Emerging Technology. (2023, June 14). *The surprising power of next-word prediction: Large language models, explained*.

Chauncey, S. A., & McKenna, H. P. (2023). An exploration of the potential of large language models to enable cognitive flexibility in AI-augmented learning environments. In K. K. Arai (Ed.), *Proceedings of the Future Technologies Conference (FTC) 2023, Vol 4*. https://doi.org/10.1007/978-3-031-47448-4_11

Chen, X., Xie, H., Zou, D., & Hwang, G.-J. (2020). Application and theory gaps during the rise of artificial intelligence in education. *Computers and Education: Artificial Intelligence, 1*, 100002. https://doi.org/10.1016/j.caeai.2020.100002

Chien-Chang, L., Huang, A., & Lu, O. (2023). Artificial intelligence in intelligent tutoring systems toward sustainable education: a systematic review. *Smart Learning Environments, 10*(41). https://doi.org/10.1186/s40561-023-00260-y

Damşa, C. I., Kirschner, P. A., Andriessen, J. E. B., Erkens, G., & Sins, P. H. M. (2010). Shared epistemic agency: An empirical study of an emergent construct. *Journal of the Learning Sciences, 19*(2), 143–186.

Ding, L., Li, T., Jiang, S., & Gapud, A. (2023). Students' perceptions of using ChatGPT in a physics class as a virtual tutor. *International Journal of Educational Technology in Higher Education, 20*(1), 1–18.

Dodge, B. (1995). WebQuests: A technique for Internet-based learning, *Distance Educator,* 1(2), 10–13.

Drake, D. (2024, January 15). *AI and you: Learn to be the human in the loop.* Wharton Global Youth Program. https://globalyouth.wharton.upenn.edu/articles/science-technology/ai-and-you-learn-to-be-the-human-in-the-loop/

Engel, S. (2015). *The hungry mind: The origins of curiosity in childhood.* Harvard University Press.

Facione, P. A. (2011). *Critical thinking: What it is and why it counts.* Insight Assessment.

Fisher, D., & Frey, N. (2021). *Better learning through structured teaching: A framework for the gradual release of responsibility* (3rd ed.). ASCD.

Fisher, D., Frey, N., Almarode, J., Barbee, K., Amador-Valerio, O., & Assof, J. (2023). *The teacher clarity playbook, grades K-12: A hands-on guide to creating learning intentions and success criteria for organized, effective instruction* (2nd ed.). Corwin.

Fisher, D., Frey, N., & Rothenberg, C. (2008). *Content area conversations: How to plan discussion-based lessons for diverse language learners.* ASCD.

FitzHenry, S., & Wilkens, K. (2017). Supermoons cause tidal waves! *School Library Journal, 63*(6), 20–21.

Flavell, J. H. (1979). Metacognition and cognitive monitoring. A new area of cognitive-development inquiry. *American Psychologist, 34*(10), 906–911.

Flower, L. (1990). Negotiating academic discourse. In L. Flower, V. Stein, J. Ackerman, M. J. Kantz, K. McCormick, & W. C. Peck (Eds.), *Reading-to-write: Exploring a cognitive and social process* (pp. 221–252). Oxford University Press.

Fordham, N. W. (2006). Crafting questions that address comprehension strategies in content reading. *Journal of Adolescent & Adult Literacy, 49*(5), 390–396. https://doi.org/10.1598/JAAL.49.5.3

Gentner, D., & Markman, A. B. (1997). Structure mapping in analogy and similarity. *American Psychologist, 52*(1), 45–56.

Gogoshin, D. L. (2025). A way forward for responsibility in the age of AI. *Inquiry, 68*(4), 1164–1197.

Gummer, E.S., & Mandinach, E.B. (2015). Building a conceptual framework for data literacy. *Teachers College Record, 117,* 1–22.

Gupta, P., Nguyen, T. N., Gonzalez, C., & Woolley, A.W. (2025). Fostering collective intelligence in human–AI collaboration: Laying the groundwork for COHUMAIN. *Topics in Cognitive Science, 17,* 189–216.

Hall, T. E., Meyer, A., & Rose, D. H. (2015). *Universal design for learning in the classroom: Practical applications.* Guilford Press.

Hargrave, M., Fisher, D., & Frey, N. (2025). *The artificial intelligence playbook: Time-saving tools for teachers that make learning more engaging* (2nd ed.). Corwin.

Harris, P. (2015). What children learn from questioning. *Educational Leadership, 73*(1), 24–29.

Hattie, J., & Timperley, H. (2007). The power of feedback. *Review of Educational Research, 77*(1), 81–112. https://doi.org/10.3102/003465430298487

Hedefalk, M., & Sumpter, L. (2025). Young children's ethical reasoning about sharing: An analytical tool. *For the Learning of Mathematics, 45*(1), 8–13.

Hobbs, R. (2020). Propaganda in an age of algorithmic personalization: Expanding literacy research and practice. *Reading Research Quarterly, 55*(3), 521–533.

Holmes, W., Bialik, M., & Fadel, C. (2019). *Artificial intelligence in education: Promises and implications for teaching and learning.* Center for Curriculum Redesign.

Huang, X., Xu, W., & Liu, R. (2025). Effects of intelligent tutoring systems on educational

REFERENCES

outcomes: Evidence from a comprehensive analysis. *International Journal of Distance Education Technologies, 23*(1), 1–25.

Jonassen, D. H. (2011). *Learning to solve problems: A handbook for designing problem-solving learning environments*. Routledge.

Khan, S. (2024). *Brave new words: How AI will revolutionize education (and why that's a good thing)*. Viking.

Kimes, M. (2024, December 29). *Navigating the future of search: The rise of GenAI vs. traditional search engines*. LinkedIn. https://www.linkedin.com/

Kuhn, D. (2005). What needs to be mastered in mastery of scientific method? *Psychological Science, 16*(11), 873–874. https://doi.org/10.1111/j.1467-9280.2005.01630.x

Lamnina, M., & Chase, C. C. (2021). Uncertain instruction: effects on curiosity, learning, and transfer. *Instructional Science, 49*(5), 661–685.

Lee, D.-C., & Chang, C.-Y. (2025). Evaluating self-directed learning competencies in digital learning environments: A meta-analysis. *Education & Information Technologies, 30*(6), 6847–6868.

Lee, K., Tsai, P.-S., Chai, C. S., & Koh, J. H. L. (2014). Perception of learning with technology. *Journal of Computer Assisted Learning, 30*, 425–437.

Leung, R., Yu, C., Cohen, R., & Young, M. (2021). Privacy literacy and education for youth in the digital age: A systematic literature review. *Journal of the Association for Information Science and Technology, 72*(2), 224–239.

Livingstone, S., Stoilova, M., & Nandagiri, R. (2019). *Children's data and privacy online: Growing up in a digital age*. London School of Economics and Political Science. https://www.lse.ac.uk/

Luckin, R., Holmes, W., Griffiths, M., & Forcier, L. B. (2022). *Intelligence unleashed: An argument for AI in education* (2nd ed.). Pearson.

Means, B. (2010). Technology and education change: Focus on student learning. *Journal of Research on Technology in Education, 42*(3), 285–307.

Mejeh, M., & Rehm, M. (2024). Taking adaptive learning in educational settings to the next level: Leveraging natural language processing for improved personalization. *Educational Technology Research & Development, 72*(3), 1597–1621.

Mercer, N., & Howe, C. (2012). Explaining the dialogic processes of teaching and learning: The value and potential of sociocultural theory. *Learning, Culture, and Social Interaction, 1*(1), 12–21.

Merga, M. K., & Mat Roni, S. (2025). School library professionals' perceptions of students' digital information literacy. *Journal of Library Administration, 65*(4), 397–411.

Miao, F., & Holmes, W. (2023). *Guidance for generative AI in education and research*. UNESCO. https://doi.org/10.54675/EWZM9535

Michaels, S., O'Connor, C., & Resnick, L. B. (2008). Deliberative discourse idealized and realized: Accountable talk in the classroom and in civic life. *Studies in Philosophy and Education, 27*(4), 283–297.

Minigan, A., Westbrook, S., Rothstein, D., & Santana, L. (2017). Stimulating and sustaining inquiry with students' questions. *Social Education 81*(5), 268–272.

Mollick, E. (2024). *Co-intelligence: Living and working with AI*. Little, Brown Spark.

Moran, K. (2024, May 24). *CARE: Structure for crafting AI prompts*. Nielsen Norman Group. https://www.nngroup.com/articles/careful-prompts/

National Center for Systematic Improvement. (2021). *Essential elements of comprehensive data literacy*. WestEd. https://ncsi.wested.org/resource/essential-elements-of-comprehensive-data-literacy/

National Research Council. (2000). *How people learn: Brain, mind, experience, and school*. National Academies Press. https://nap.nationalacademies.org/catalog/9853/how-people-learn-brain-mind-experience-and-school-expanded-edition

Nielsen Norman Group. (2023, March 19). *Anthropomorphism and AI: Why we attribute human traits to machines*. https://www.nngroup.com/articles/anthropomorphism/

OECD. (2025). *Empowering learners for the age of AI: An AI literacy framework for primary and *secondary education* (Review draft). Paris. https://ailiteracyframework.org

Ostroff, W. L. (2020). Empowering children through dialogue and discussion. In *Educational Leadership, 77*(7), 14–20.

Panadero, E. (2016). Is it safe? Social, interpersonal, and human effects of peer assessment. In G. T. L. Brown & L. R. Harris (Eds.), *Handbook of human and social conditions in assessment* (pp. 247–265). Routledge/Taylor & Francis.

Panadero, E. (2017). A review of self-regulated learning: Six models and four directions for research. *Frontiers in Psychology, 8*, 422. https://doi.org/10.3389/fpsyg.2017.00422

Raphael, T. E., Highfield, K., & Au, K. H. (2006). *QAR now: A powerful and practical framework that develops comprehension and higher-level thinking in all students*. Scholastic.

Richland, L. E., & McDonough, I. K. (2010). Learning by analogy: Discriminating between potential analogs. *Contemporary Educational Psychology, 35*(1), 28–43. https://doi.org/10.1016/j.cedpsych.2009.09.001

Roll, I., & Winne, P. H. (2015). Understanding, evaluating, and supporting self-regulated learning using learning analytics. *Journal of Learning Analytics, 2*(1), 7–12. https://doi.org/10.18608/jla.2015.21.2

Rothstein, D., & Santana, L. (2011). *Make just one change: Teach students to ask their own questions*. Harvard Education Press.

Schleicher, A. (2018, November 12). Educating students for their future, not our past. *Teacher Magazine*. https://www.teachermagazine.com/au_en/articles/educating-students-for-their-future-not-our-past

Schraw, G., & Dennison, R. S. (1994). Assessing metacognitive awareness. *Contemporary Educational Psychology, 19*(4), 460–475.

Siegler, R. S., & Chen, Z. (2008). Differentiation and integration: Guiding principles for analyzing cognitive change. *Developmental Science, 11*, 433–448. https://doi.org/10.1111/j.1467-7687.2008.00689.x

Spiro, R., Coulson, R., Feltovich, P. J., & Anderson, D. (1988). Cognitive flexibility theory: Advanced knowledge acquisition in ill-structured domains. *Cognitive Science, 12*, 544–557.

Teplitski, M., Irani, T., Krediet, C. J., Di Cesare, M., & Marvasi, M. (2018). Student-generated pre-exam questions is an effective tool for participatory learning: A case study from ecology of waterborne pathogens course. *Journal of Food Science Education, 17*(3), 76–84. https://doi.org/10.1111/1541-4329.12129

USC Center for Generative AI and Society. (2024, February 5). How teachers make ethical judgments when using AI in the classroom. *USC Today*. https://today.usc.edu/ai-in-the-classroom-how-teachers-make-ethical-judgments/

Van de Pol, J., Volman, M., & Beishuizen, J. (2010). Scaffolding in teacher–student interaction: A decade of research. *Educational Psychology Review, 22*(3), 271–296. https://doi.org/10.1007/s10648-010-9127-6

Vygotsky, L. S. (1978). *Mind in society: The development of higher psychological processes*. Harvard University Press.

Watson, A. P. (2024). Hallucinated citation analysis: Delving into student-submitted AI-generated sources at the University of Mississippi. *The Serials Librarian, 85*(5/6), 172–180.

Wegerif, R. (2013). *Dialogic: Education for the internet age*. Routledge.

Wineburg, S., McGrew, S., Breakstone, J., & Ortega, T. (2016–2020). *Evaluating information: The cornerstone of civic online reasoning*. Stanford History Education Group. https://cor.inquirygroup.org/curriculum/

World Economic Forum. (2025). *Future of jobs report 2025*. https://www.weforum.org/reports/the-future-of-jobs-report-2025/

World Economic Forum. (2025). *The reskilling revolution: Transforming education, skills and learning*. https://initiatives.weforum.org/reskilling-revolution/home

Xie, H., Chu, H. C., Hwang, G. J., & Wang, C. C. (2019). Trends and development in technology-enhanced

REFERENCES

adaptive/personalized learning: A systematic review of journal publications from 2007 to 2017. *Computers & Education*, *140*, Article 103599. https://doi.org/10.1016/j.compedu.2019.103599

Yang, Y., & Xia, N. (2023). Enhancing students' metacognition via AI-driven educational support systems. *International Journal of Emerging Technologies in Learning*, *18*(24), 133–148.

Yeager, D. (2024). *10 to 25: The science of motivating young people: A groundbreaking approach to leading the next generation—And making your own life easier*. Avid Reader Press/Simon & Schuster.

Zhai, C., Wibowo, S., & Li, L. D. (2024). The effects of over-reliance on AI dialogue systems on students' cognitive abilities: a systematic review. *Smart Learning Environments*, *11*(1), 28–37. https://doi.org/10.1186/s40561-024-00316-7

Zhong, B., Liu, X., & Li, X. (2024). Effects of reverse engineering pedagogy on students' learning performance in STEM education: The bridge-design project as an example. *Heliyon*, *10*(2). https://doi.org/10.1016/j.heliyon.2024.e24278

Zohar, A., & David, A. B. (2009). Paving a clear path in a thick forest: A conceptual analysis of a metacognitive component. *Metacognition and Learning*, *4*(3), 177–195. https://doi.org/10.1007/s11409-009-9044-6

INDEX

Adaptive learning programs, 2, 91–92
Adaptive platforms, 5, 27–31
"AI-as-Advisor" protocol, 23
AI-based Socratic tools, 13
AI Helper Station, 23
AI-supported learning environments, 119
Analogical reasoning, 111
Anchor Quest, 111–114
Artificial intelligence (AI)
   K–12 classrooms, 151
   literacy, 3–4
   PK–12 students, 1
   revolution, 45
   teaching, 2–3. *See also* Teaching *about* AI; Teaching *for* AI; Teaching *with* AI
Artificial Intelligence Playbook (Hargrave et al.), 3

Bing Chat, 72
Bloom, B., 13

Chatbot, 38
   AI systems, 65
   and image generators, 45
   long-term assignment, 101
   structured experiences, 3
   student thinking, 22
ChatGPT, 1, 3, 22, 37, 72
Chicken Clicking (Willis), 35
Civic Online Reasoning model (COR), 71
Civic systems, 42
Clarity Quest, 115–118
Closed questions, 56
Cognitive flexibility, 46, 90–94
Cognitive processes, 56
Cognitive science, 14
Co-Intelligence (Mollick), 151
Collaborative learning community, 23
Collective intelligence, 2, 22–26
Color-coded system, 50
Comparative reasoning, principles of, 119
Compare Quest, 119–122
Content learning, 61

Critical cognitive skills, 104
Critical interpretation, 76–79
Critical thinking skill, 90
Critique Quest, 123–126
Curiosity, 2, 4, 45, 46, 49, 73, 80–83, 90, 143, 144, 151

Data exploration, 52, 53
Data literacy, 52–55
Data management, 52
Data usage, 52
Decision-making, 3, 13, 25, 32, 48, 53, 54, 95–98, 101, 104–108
Deep learning, 52, 84, 111
DeepL/Google Translate, 20
Dennison, R. S., 84
Digital literacy, 36
Ding, L., 17
DreamBox, 27
Dual coding station, 14
Duolingo, 27

Educational research supports, 12, 111
Elaboration station, 14
Electric bike, 17
Ethical reasoning skills, 95–99
Evidence-based critique, 124
Evidence-based strategy, 14

Fisher, D., 68
FitzHenry, S., 71
Flavell, J. H., 84
Frey, N., 68

Generative models, 2, 5, 7–11
Graphic organizers, 49, 50, 78, 145
Growth Quest, 127–130
Growth-supporting feedback, 127

Hattie, J., 127
Holmes, W., 17
Human intelligence skills, 3, 65, 151

Human-in-the-loop experiences, 17–21
Human–Technology–Human (H–T–H) formula, 17

If-then logic algorithm, 27
Industrial Revolution, 45
Information literacy (IL), 48–51, 71
Intelligent tutoring systems (ITSs), 12–13, 27–28
iReady, 27

Khanmigo, 22, 27
Knowledge-building community, 23

Learner
  identity interviews, 13
  profile system, 28
Learning
  playlist, 13
  process, 100
Level-Up Quest, 131–134

Metacognition, 84–89
Mission Quest, 135–138

Natural language processing (NLP), 7
Neuroscience, 14
Nielsen Norman Group, 36
North Carolina Department of Public Instruction, 105

Open questions, 56
Organisation for Economic Co-operation and Development, 41

Pattern-based tool, 9
Peer-to-peer activity, 13
Perplexity, 72
Personalized learning plans, 13
Personalized mastery-based learning, 2, 12–16
Perspective Quest, 139–142
Problem-based learning, 135
Problem-solving skill, 90
Prompt engineering, 3, 61–64
Proximal development theory, 131
Public service announcement (PSA), 39
Purpose-driven learning, 135

Question-answer relationship (QAR) framework, 58
Question Formation Technique, 57
Questioning, 3, 56–60

Reflection and improvement, 52
Responsible AI, 36, 73, 106, 107
Retrieval practice station, 14
Reverse Quest, 143–146

Right-Sizing Quest, 147–150
Ross, D., 68

Schraw, G., 84
Self-assessment, 85, 86, 123
Self-directed growth, 84
Self-directed learning (SDL) skills, 100
Self-monitoring, 115, 127
Self-regulation, 32, 100–103, 123, 127
Socratic method, 12
Spaced repetition station, 14
Spotify, 27
Student Online Personal Information Protection Act (SOPIPA), 33
Support learning, 48, 61
Surface-level responses, 76
  Surface-level traits, 119

Teachable Machine (Google), 8
Teaching *about* AI
  adaptive platforms, 5, 27–31
  collective intelligence, 22–26
  common classroom applications, 33
  data collection and personalization process, 32
  extension/adaptation idea, 34–35
  generative models, 7–11
  grade band, 35
  human–AI collaboration, 6
  human-in-the-loop, 5, 17–21
  limitations, 36–40
  personalized mastery-based learning, 12–16
  self-regulation and decision-making skills, 32
  and society, 41–44
  strategy in action, 34
  tools, 32
Teaching *for* AI
  chatbots, 45
  cognitive flexibility, 90–94
  critical interpretation, 76–79
  curiosity, 80–83
  data literacy, 52–55
  dialogue, 65–70
  ethical reasoning, 95–99
  human brain, 46
  image generators, 45
  Industrial Revolution, 45
  information literacy (IL), 48–51
  metacognition, 84–89
  prompt engineering, 61–64
  questioning, 56–60
  self-regulation, 100–103
  skill types, 45, 47 (figure)
  teacher decision-making, 104–108
  verification, 71–75

Teaching *with* AI
    Anchor Quest, 111–114
    categories, 109
    Clarity Quest, 115–118
    Compare Quest, 119–122
    Critique Quest, 123–126
    Growth Quest, 127–130
    learning outcomes, 109
    Level-Up Quest, 131–134
    Mission Quest, 135–138
    Perspective Quest, 139–142
    Reverse Quest, 143–146
    Right-Sizing Quest, 147–150
    structured learning experience, 110
    students' independent learning, 109
The Technology Tail (Cook), 35
Think-aloud strategy, 9, 50
TikTok, 27
Timperley, H., 127

UNESCO, *Guidance for Generative AI in Education,* 53
Universal Design for Learning, principles of, 131, 147
USC Center for Generative AI and Society (2024), 104

Verification, 71–75

WebQuests, 3
Whale-watching, 1
Wilkens, K., 71
World Economic Forum, *Future of Jobs Report* (2024), 45

Xia, N., 84

Yang, Y., 84
Yeager, D., 100
YouTube, 27

Take your teaching further

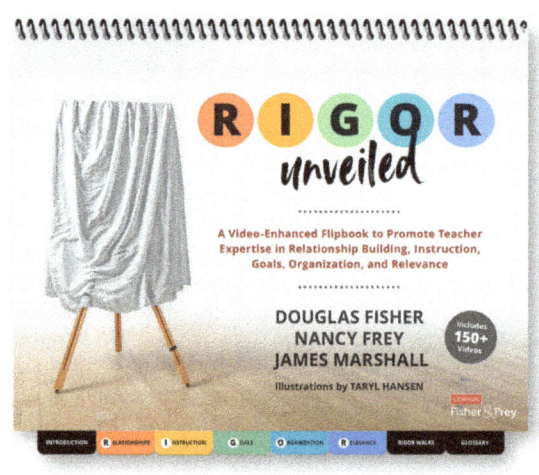

You may also be interested in...

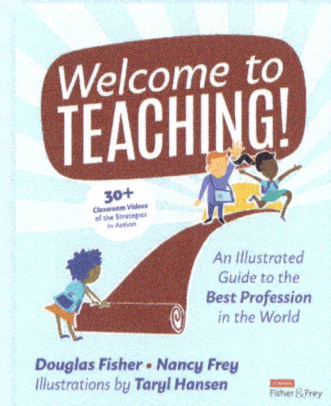

To learn more, visit corwin.com

CORWIN
Fisher & Frey

Deepen Your Team's Learning with Workshops by Douglas Fisher and Nancy Frey

Empower educators and elevate student success through evidence-based professional learning workshops, inspired by Fisher & Frey's best-selling books. With these evidence-based and customizable workshops, educators strengthen their knowledge, skills, and practice, leading to measurable student growth and achievement.

- Customize your learning with workshops that adapt to your goals and priorities.
- Access our expert-curated resources and strategies rooted in decades of proven research.
- Inspire your educators with professional learning designed to make a lasting impact.

Popular professional learning services include:

- PLC+
- Teacher Clarity
- R.I.G.O.R. Walks
- Teaching Students to Drive Their Learning

Need more information?
Visit www.corwin.com/fisherandfreypd for full listing of services.

CORWIN

To help every educator help every student

We believe that every single student deserves a great education

We believe that knowing our impact is both a privilege and a responsibility

We believe that a fair, stable, and thriving society is built on education